YOUR NEXT PLAY

HOW TO BUILD PURPOSE, IDENTITY, AND DIRECTION BEYOND SPORTS.

DEJI OLAJIDE

FOREWORD BY JON DECUIR

ISBN: 979-8-9879166-7-4
Published by Session 5 Institute
www.session5institute.com

Cover Designer: Quanesha Moore

Unless otherwise indicated, all scripture quotations are
taken from New International Version®, NIV®. Copyright
© 1973, 1978, 1984, 2011 by Biblica, Inc.™

For permissions or inquiries, contact:
deji@session5institute.com

DEDICATION

To my parents, Dr. Emmanuel Olajide and Winifred Olajide, for your unwavering love, discipline, and example. Everything I build stands on what you poured into me.

And to my mentor, coach, and pastor, Jonathan DeCuir, for sharpening my vision, strengthening my faith, and teaching me that purpose is always bigger than the platform.

CONTENTS

FOREWARD

BY JONATHAN DECUIR

"Preparation is faith dressed in work clothes. When you start building before you see the rain, God meets you in motion."

There's a moment every athlete knows, but few prepare for: the last whistle. The lights dim, the locker room grows quiet, and the rhythm that ordered your days, practice, film, weights, team meetings, fades into a silence that can feel like free falling. For too many, that silence becomes a fog of questions: Who am I without the jersey? Where do I place my drive now? What's my next play when the playbook I've lived by is no longer in my hands? This book is for that moment.

I've had the privilege of mentoring Deji for six years, long enough to watch raw talent become tested character, and ambition mature into assignment. He was a standout football player in high school and at Azusa Pacific University, but what sets

Deji apart isn't what he achieved on the field, it's what he built afterward. He chose to prepare before the rain. While others waited for clarity to arrive, Deji started building clarity with the same intensity he brought to "two-a-days."

He became a student of growth, reliable, consistent, unshakably committed to daily, unglamorous reps that most people skip. I've watched him get up early to read, to plan, to learn new skills, to serve other athletes, to network with humility, and to set goals that had nothing to do with applause and everything to do with purpose.

That's why *Your Next Play* carries weight. It isn't theory, it's a blueprint born of sweat, humility, and tested habits. Deji writes as a living example of what to do when the season shifts and the lights go out. He speaks to high school and college athletes who sense the clock winding down and wonder, "What now?" He answers with clarity, courage, and a practical path forward. Let me say this plainly: Deji's growth has been leaps and bounds, not by accident but by intention. He has trained his life the way great athletes train their bodies, on purpose and with purpose.

Your Next Play is a book about identity, but it's also a book about decisions. It's about how purpose is discovered in motion, how preparation is the strongest signal you can send to your future, and how the same discipline that made you a competitor can make you a builder, a leader, a creator, and a contributor long after the crowd goes home.

Athletes, hear me: the end of your career is not the end of your calling. It's a handoff. And handoffs require timing, trust, and strong footing. This book will help you place your feet.

WHAT I'VE WITNESSED UP CLOSE

I've watched Deji do what many talk about, but few practice: He chose values before victories. When a door opened that didn't fit his long-term direction, he didn't chase the spotlight, he stayed true to the assignment.

He built transferable skills. He turned communication, time management, project planning, relationship stewardship, and financial wisdom into daily drills, not occasional wishes.

He served others while he was still finding his way. That posture sharpened his own purpose.

He kept excellent company. He curated a circle that pulled him forward, not sideways. He learned that your circle is a current, and he chose the current that carried him toward a meaningful future.

He prepared before the opportunity. He wrote the plan, refined the résumé, scheduled the call, showed up early, and did it consistently. He didn't wait for rain. He started building the ark.

That's who is writing to you. Not a distant commentator, but a teammate who has run the route and made the cut when it mattered.

WHY THIS BOOK MATTERS RIGHT NOW

The transition out of sport is one of the most under-coached seasons in a young athlete's life. We coach the sprint and ignore the baton pass. We celebrate signing day and skip planning day. We tell you to "work hard", but don't teach you how to convert grind into growth when the scoreboard changes.

Deji fills that gap with a clear promise: A blueprint for athletes to discover purpose, build transferable skills, and launch their next season with clarity.He is not asking you to abandon everything that made you who you are; he's showing you how to redeploy it.

The same intensity that powered you through early lifts can power you through early classes, certifications, internships, or business plans. The same resilience that battled injury can fuel recovery, reinvention, and leadership. The same teamwork that bound you to a locker room can build networks that open doors you didn't know existed.

FROM LOCKER ROOM TO LAUNCHPAD

I remember a conversation with Deji after a tough decision he had to make. He could have chosen easy attention. Instead, he chose alignment. We talked about how suggestions can derail purpose and how one voice in the wrong season can make you doubt what you know to be true. He guarded his heart, slowed down, and let time reveal substance. That maturity is woven throughout this book. He'll help you pause when pressure shouts, "Decide fast," and he'll guide you to decide well.

He'll also challenge your circle. Your circle is a current, not just company. It is pulling you forward, drifting you sideways, or dragging you under, but it is doing something. Deji will help you choose the current that carries you into your calling.

PREPARATION IS YOUR SIGNAL

One of the most powerful ideas you'll encounter here is simple and strong: preparation moves the hand of God on your life and it moves opportunity toward you. Start where you are. Write the plan. Draft the email. Enroll in the class. Shadow the leader. Serve the mission. Build before the rain. The moment you begin to prepare, momentum begins to form. It's amazing how often "chance" favors those who were already in motion.

Deji's life bears this out. He didn't wait for a big break; he became ready for the breaks that came. He learned that readiness is not luck, it's stewardship.

MY CONFIDENCE IN THE AUTHOR AND IN YOU

As Lead Pastor at Victory Bible Church and CEO of Session 5 Institute, I've dedicated my life to helping people discover their purpose and walk it out with integrity. I don't lend my voice to every project. I gladly lend it to this one.

I believe in this book because I believe in the man who wrote it. I have seen Deji, year after year, choose growth over comfort, character over clout, and purpose over pressure. He is reliable. He is passionate about athletes finding who they are beyond the game and he has earned the right to speak into this moment because he has lived it well.

I also believe in you. If you're holding this book, you've already taken a step many never take. You're choosing to prepare. You're choosing to build. You're choosing to lead your life instead of letting your life lead you.

Don't wait for the perfect plan to start. Start, and your plan will become clearer. Don't wait for someone else to name your future. Speak life over it. Don't hand your identity to applause or opinions. Anchor it in values and vision that hold when seasons change.

Your next season is not a consolation prize, it's a calling and you are ready.Turn the page. Study the blueprint. Run the play. Build before the rain. Your next play begins now.

— Jonathan DeCuir M.Div.

Lead Pastor, Victory Bible Church

CEO, Session 5 Institute

INTRODUCTION

Every athlete remembers the moment the game ends.The final whistle blows. The crowd begins to thin out. The field that once felt electric grows quiet. For years, your life has revolved around practice schedules, workouts, meetings, and game days. Then one day, it stops.

No one really talks about that moment.You train your body to endure pain. You train your mind to compete. You train your discipline to show up when it matters, but very few people train you for what happens after the uniform comes off.

When the season ends for good, the silence can feel louder than any stadium ever did. That silence is where the real questions begin.

THIS BOOK IS NOT REALLY ABOUT SPORTS.

Sports is the backdrop. It is where many of these lessons surfaced, but it is not the point. The point is purpose.

Growing up, I would often hear people say, "Everyone has a purpose." It sounded inspiring, but it also sounded distant. I remember thinking, *Okay… but what is mine?* Where do you find it? How do you know when you've discovered it? And what if you miss it?

Purpose always felt mysterious to me. Like something reserved for people who had it all figured out. It felt far away, like a destination on a map I couldn't quite see. I didn't know why I was here. I didn't know what I was supposed to build and I didn't know what contribution I was meant to make. What I did know was how to perform.

SPORTS BECAME MY LOVE EARLY.

It started on the track in elementary school. I still remember the first time I picked up a ball and felt something click. Football, in particular, felt different. It felt like more than a game. It felt like identity. It felt like strength. It felt like manhood. The discipline, the physicality, the brotherhood, the community, all of it pulled me in.

Through middle school and into high school, the game shaped my world. It gave me structure. It gave me direction. It gave me something to aim at, but the journey was not a straight line. There were highs and lows. There were health challenges that forced perspective. There was the disappointment of not going Division 1 when I thought I would. There were college seasons filled with both achievement and frustration. Wins that felt like validation and losses that felt personal. Looking back, I can see how deeply I had connected my sense of worth to performance.

And then, eventually, the game ended. Not in one dramatic moment. Not in some movie-scene fashion. It ended the way it ends for almost everyone, quietly and inevitably. That is when I realized something important. The struggle most athletes face after sports is not about failing, it is about not being prepared for transition.

Sports gave me direction, structure, and measurable wins and losses. It gave me something to chase and because it gave me clarity, I started to mistake it for purpose. No one had taught me how to separate who I was from what I did or showed me how to rediscover purpose when the platform changed.

I quickly learned when you are not clear on who you are, it becomes easy to compare. I found myself constantly measuring my life against other people's lives. Maybe I should be like him. Maybe I should do what they're doing. That looks impressive. That looks meaningful. That looks important. Instead of honoring my own path, I diminished it. I minimized what I had accomplished and magnified what others had done. In my mind, their lives always looked bigger. More significant. More purposeful.

Without a sense of purpose, I wasn't building toward something. I was reacting to what everyone else seemed to be building. I was running, but I wasn't sure where I was going and that is exhausting.

Living without clarity felt like running on a treadmill. Constant motion. No real progress. I was working hard, showing up, doing what was expected, but internally I felt unsure, isolated, and confused. I didn't have a clear vision of where my life was headed, so of course I didn't know what steps to take. When sports ended, that confusion became louder because if the game was not my purpose, then what was?

If any of that feels familiar, you're probably in it right now.

Maybe your sport already ended. Maybe you can see the end coming. Maybe you're still playing, but you know it won't last forever. Or maybe this isn't even about sports for you. Maybe it's graduation. Maybe it's a job that didn't turn out how you expected or a dream that quietly shifted. Whatever it is, the experience feels similar.

One day you realize the structure that used to hold your life together isn't there anymore. The routine changes, expectations change and the way people see you starts to change. If you're honest, the way you see yourself changes too. That's the part no one really talks about. When something that shaped your identity ends, it leaves space and space can feel uncomfortable. It can feel like uncertainty or that you're behind, even when you're not.

I didn't struggle because I wasn't capable. I struggled because I didn't know how to think about my life without football at the center of it. If you've ever found yourself asking, "If this isn't it anymore, then what is?", you understand what I was feeling.

The game may have ended. That doesn't mean your purpose did, but finding it requires more than motivation. It requires clarity.

That's why this book exists. I wrote this book, not because I have all the answers or because I mastered transition overnight, but because I had to walk through it. Along the way, I learned principles that changed everything for me and my hope is it changes things for you too.

If you are reading this and you feel stuck, unsure, restless, or even strangely numb, you are not weak. You are not behind. You are not broken. You are in between plays and in between plays is where decisions get made.

Your Next Play book is built like a playbook. Each chapter is a play, and every play moves you forward. We'll start by helping you get honest about where you are. Not where you wish you were, not where people expect you to be, but where you actually stand. Then we'll deal with what often holds people back. The pain. The comparison. The identity confusion that shows up when the uniform comes off.

From there, we'll rebuild. You'll learn how to develop a stronger sense of identity, carry the lessons sports gave you into real life, and step into new experiences that stretch you. Your next opportunity is likely tied to relationships. So, learning how to build genuine connections, create value, and grow your network matters. In addition to building connections and a network with others, I'll close the book by talking about the greatest connection of all, our spiritual one.

Throughout this book, I will reference my relationship with God and the role faith has played in my journey. Scripture may be woven in where it shaped how I think and how I moved forward. At the same time, I recognize that not everyone reading this shares the same beliefs. Whether you are strong in your faith, exploring it, unsure about it, or do not claim one at all, you are welcome here. The principles in this book are practical. My faith informs them, but you can engage with them wherever you stand.

At the end of each chapter, you'll find something called Run This Play. These are not throwaway questions. They're exercises and prompts designed to help you apply what you're reading. Reading without reflection rarely creates change. Movement does. So, I wanted to encourage you to lean in and get ready for your next play.

PLAY #1
START WHERE YOU ARE

Every GPS works the same way. It doesn't start by asking where you're going, it starts by asking where you are. Without that, the directions don't work.

This chapter is that moment. The starting point. Before you think about purpose, identity, or what's next, you have to tell the truth about where you're standing right now. This isn't about judgment or regret. It's about honesty, because the only way forward is to start where you are. For me, that moment came when I realized I had been moving through life without really feeling anything at all.

WHEN IT HITS

While I was in college, I remember going to visit a significant friend of mine in prison. This is someone I had done life with, built memories with, and cared about deeply. I visited him several times and surprisingly, what I remember the most was how numb I felt. No empathy, no compassion, nothing. I knew, logically, that his situation should have shaken me. Instead, I sat across from him, carrying on conversation like nothing was wrong, completely disconnected from the weight of where we were.

It wasn't until after several visits that I realized he wasn't the only one in prison, but I was too. While I was physically sitting in the prison's visitor room across from my friend, my emotions were locked away. If this sounds familiar, if you're moving through life numb or disconnected, it may be a sign that you're in bondage too. As a result of this revelation, I decided at that moment that I would begin to work on feeling again.

While I can't pinpoint when I stopped feeling, the earliest I can recall is when I started playing football at a young age. Over the years, I was conditioned not to show any emotions. I couldn't cry when I got injured or express any disappointment when I made a bad play, lost, or didn't get to play enough. Early on, the narrative "be a man" was ingrained in me and that often meant suppressing my emotions. Maybe you can relate.

As I began to process my experience visiting my friend in prison and the full range of emotions that came with it, I learned that it was safe to do so. Feeling sadness, pain, and hurt was difficult and vulnerable, but more dangerous when avoided. That season of deep work pushed me outside of my box. Eventually, I found myself saying things like, "Hey, in life you will have emotions and they don't have to be bad. They are natural. Accept them for where they are." I was growing and accepting my emotions. Starting where I was really prepared me for the next season I didn't even know was coming. Just a year later, my senior year in college, I faced the devastation of saying goodbye to the game I played and loved.

The reality of my football career ending didn't hit me all at once. It hit me over the week after our final game of the season. On Monday following the game, our head coach gathered us together and had a conversation that set the tone for what became one of the biggest transitions of my life. He said something like, "this sport was never your purpose, it was your platform to display who you are. Being an athlete is what you did, but being a leader is who you are…now go and lead in life…"

His words were encouraging, but they did not make the pain and questions go away. If anything, they confirmed what I was already starting to feel. One chapter of my life had ended and I had no clear picture of what the next one was supposed to look like.

THE QUESTIONS NOBODY PREPARES YOU FOR

For as long as I could remember, my days had been full. Between class, practice, meetings, workouts, and games, football didn't just take up my time, it gave my life structure. Then suddenly, there was nothing. No practice. No meetings. No schedule telling me where to be. I remember thinking, *What am I supposed to do with all of this free time?* There was so much of it and for the first time, it didn't feel freeing. It felt confusing.

Later in the semester, while at home, the house where all the football players stayed and hung out, more questions began to flood in. I just so happened to be alone because my course load was much lighter than my teammates and I remember the deep sense of loneliness and confusion I felt. I was lost. I remember thinking, *"Oh, crap! What am I supposed to do now? Who am I now? What will my life be like now? How will my life's routine be structured without being centered on sports?"*

The more the questions came, the more reality set in and the heavier everything felt. Confusion turned into loneliness. Loneliness turned into grief. And before I knew it, I felt devastated and depressed in a way I wasn't prepared for. I'm not afraid to admit that I even cried about it.

To this day, whenever I need to relieve stress, I get in my car and just drive around. I recall this was one of those moments. I had a 2006 Toyota Corolla. It wasn't in the best shape, but it got me where I needed to go. At the time, I lived in Glendora, CA, a city right at the base of the Foothill Mountains. I was driving around and eventually found myself going up the canyon until I found a lookout over the city. I pulled over, parked, and just cried. I totally broke down in a way I don't ever remember breaking down before in life.

It's difficult to explain the pain of an ended sports career to someone who's never lived it. When you've spent your whole life chasing the dream of playing at the highest level, and it all comes to an end, it feels like a breakup. You've poured your time, energy, and heart into something and suddenly, it's gone.

Sitting there in my car, all I could think was, I gave everything I had to this. What do I have now? What's next for me?

Maybe you've felt something like that too. Maybe the uniform came off, the schedule disappeared, and the questions started piling up. If so, I want you to know this: you're not strange for feeling this way. You're not weak for grieving what ended.

YOU'RE NOT THE ONLY ONE

What surprised me later was realizing that this experience wasn't unique to me or to athletes who "didn't make it." Michael Jordan, arguably the most dominant basketball player of all time, has openly admitted that when he first walked away from the game, he felt empty. Basketball had been the organizing force of his life. When it ended, he didn't know what to do with himself.

His first retirement wasn't about losing ability, it was about losing direction. Baseball wasn't a passion; it was an attempt to outrun grief. That's the part most people miss. Greatness doesn't exempt you from this moment. In some ways, it makes it harder because when the game ends, you're not just losing a career. You're losing a version of yourself the world knows how to celebrate.

Shaquille O'Neal once said that retirement was harder than he expected, not physically, but internally. When the game ended, he wasn't "the guy" anymore. He had spent decades being known, recognized, and affirmed as a basketball player. When that stopped, he had to confront a question no one prepares athletes to answer: Who are you when the uniform comes off?

That question hits harder than any defender ever could because without the jersey, the schedule, the applause, and the role, many athletes realize they've never been taught how to see themselves outside the game.

The problem isn't that athletes struggle when the game ends. The problem is pretending they shouldn't. If I'm honest, this is the part of my story I didn't plan for. Is that where you are too?

THE TRAP AFTER THE QUESTIONS

There is a moment in every transition when you have a choice. You can face reality, or you can avoid it. Avoidance is tempting, especially in seasons like this. When the game ends and the structure disappears, your mind fills the space with questions. Here are the 3 most common I've experienced and seen others ask:

What if?

Why?

What's next?

Those questions are normal in a season like this, but they can become dangerous when they are only asked in one direction. When every question looks backward and assumes something went wrong, they stop helping and start trapping you. For example, you might find yourself thinking: *What if I had made that big play in the third game of the season? Would my career still be going right now? What if I had* gone to a different school? Would things have turned out differently? What if I had played another position, or gotten more opportunities? Would I have been scouted by now? Maybe I didn't give it everything I had. Maybe I could have pushed harder or focused more.

When questions like these go unchecked, they quietly rewrite the story in your head. They turn into endless replays of what cannot be changed. Instead of helping you understand where you are, they pull you back into a past you no longer have the power to fix. When that happens, most people do not just stay stuck in their thoughts. They start finding ways to escape what they do not want to face.

I have seen athletes who refuse to accept that their career is over and instead choose to live as if it never really ended. Years later, they still walk around like they are on the team. In their minds, they are still the star athlete everyone loved. They train like a tryout is coming. They compete in recreational leagues like a championship is on the line. Everything becomes about proving they still have it.

Let's call this fantasy mode. It is a way of holding on to an identity that once gave you value, structure, and validation. From the outside, it is hard to watch. From the inside, it feels safer than letting go.

For some people, they get stuck trying to change the past. They replay moments over and over in their minds, convinced that if one thing had gone differently, everything would have worked out. One more play. One different decision. One better opportunity. They live in constant rewind, hoping the past will somehow give them another chance.

Others escape by rushing into the future. They grab onto the next thing quickly, not because it fits, but because standing still feels uncomfortable. Any movement feels better than none, even if it leads somewhere that does not actually align with who they are.

Some people numb the pain instead. They stay busy. They distract themselves. They avoid quiet moments because quiet makes the questions louder. This can look like partying, scrolling, substances, or always being on the go. It feels like relief in the moment, but the pain does not disappear. It just waits.

Then there are those who shrink. They lower their expectations. They stop dreaming. They convince themselves that wanting more is dangerous, so it is safer not to want much at all. This response is quieter, but it can be just as damaging. Those choices might feel like relief at the moment, but they come at a cost. They can derail your transition into the next season of life and damage your relationships, finances, and sense of direction.

If you ignore your reality and act like your emotions are not there, eventually something starts to break down. You can only say "I'm good" so many times before it becomes obvious that you are not. You have probably seen people like that before. They always say they are fine, but you can tell they are carrying something heavy.

The same is true here. You are not really fooling anyone when your sports career ends. People know how much you poured into your sport. They know how badly you wanted it to work out. They know you are hurting, whether you say it out loud or not.

It is okay to put on a brave face in public, but it is not okay to ignore what you are feeling completely. If you are not working through your emotions with people you trust, they do not disappear. They sit beneath the surface and slowly begin to affect every area of your life.The truth of the matter is, avoiding reality does not protect you, it simply postpones your progress.

BETWEEN PLAYS

If you are here, it does not mean you failed. It does not mean you missed your moment and it does not mean something is wrong with you. It means you are between plays.

In sports, being between plays is not a problem. It is part of the game. The whistle blows. The play ends. Everyone resets. No one panics when the ball is not moving because they understand that what happens next depends on what just ended.

LIFE WORKS THE SAME WAY.

This space you are in right now may feel uncomfortable, but it is not wasted time. It is a moment to slow down and take an honest look at where you really are, not where you thought you would be or hoped to be.

Looking back, I never would have guessed that sitting in a prison visitor room would become the starting point for one of the hardest and most important transitions of my life. At the time, I thought I was there to support someone else. I had no idea those visits would force me to face things I had been avoiding in myself.

Maybe, right now, you don't feel devastated. You may not feel broken or lost. You might even feel relieved that this chapter of your life is over or maybe you're feeling it all of it at once. Whatever you are feeling, this moment still matters.

Before you can choose your next play, you have to fully step off the field you were just on. Which means you have to be willing to stand honestly where you are. Not rushing. Not pretending. Not replaying what already ended. Consider how you handle this moment will shape every one that follows.

RUN THE PLAY

Play #1 isn't about fixing your life or figuring out what's next. It is about being honest about where you are. Before you move on, take a moment to run this play.

1. ENTER YOUR CURRENT LOCATION

Like a GPS, nothing works without an accurate starting point. Take a few minutes and answer this honestly, either in your head or on paper:

- Where am I right now in my life?
- What has ended that I may still be holding onto?
- What am I avoiding naming because it feels uncomfortable?

Do not judge your answers.

Do not try to improve them.

Just tell the truth.

2. NAME WHAT YOU'RE ACTUALLY FEELING

You don't need the perfect words. You just need honest ones.

Finish this sentence as many times as you need to:

- Right now, I feel _________ about this season.

You might feel disappointed. Relieved. Confused. Numb. Hopeful. Angry. Or a mix of all of it.

Whatever comes up is allowed. The goal is not to change how you feel. It is to acknowledge it.

3. CHECK FOR AVOIDANCE

Be real with yourself here.

Which of these do you see showing up most in your life right now?

- Living in fantasy mode or replaying the past
- Rushing into the next thing just to feel productive
- Numbing the discomfort through distractions
- Shrinking your expectations or playing small

This is not about guilt. It is about awareness. You cannot address what you refuse to see.

4. SAY IT OUT LOUD

Silence gives avoidance power.

Say this out loud to yourself, or to someone you trust:

"This is where I am right now. I don't have to like it, but I'm willing to be honest about it."

Sometimes the bravest move is simply naming reality without running from it.

PLAY #2:
LEVERAGE YOUR PAIN

Every athlete knows what film day feels like. You sit in a dark room watching plays you wish had gone differently. Missed blocks. Bad reads. Moments you want to fast-forward through. Film doesn't care how hard you tried or what you meant to do. It only shows what actually happened. Film is not there to embarrass you; it is there to make you better. It gives you leverage for the games to come.

Pain works the same way. As we've already mentioned, most people treat pain like something to avoid, numb, or ignore. Athletes are especially good at this. We are taught to push through, shake it off, and keep moving, but unexamined pain doesn't disappear. It just shows up later in different ways.

When you learn to look at pain honestly instead of running from it, it starts giving you information. It shows you what mattered, what hurt, what was exposed and what still needs attention. Pain can be leveraged for growth, clarity, and direction when you are willing to let it shape you instead of shut you down.

If Chapter 1 was about telling the truth about where you are, this chapter is about deciding what you are going to do with what hurts and I am not just talking about the pain that comes from the game ending. Some of the deepest pain we carry has nothing to do with sports at all.

A DIFFERENT KIND OF LOSS

Several years ago, I was traveling for a conference on the East Coast. I was in a city I had never spent much time in before, surrounded by history, landmarks, and people going about their lives. It also happened to be a place where some of my family lived.

One evening, I decided to visit a close family member who lived not far from where I was staying. I did not call ahead. I thought a surprise visit would be a good thing. Something meaningful. I pictured a quick catch-up, a hug, maybe a conversation we had not had in a long time.

The weather had been warm all day, so I stepped off the train dressed for summer. Within seconds, a sudden storm rolled in. Heavy rain. No warning. No umbrella. I ran through unfamiliar streets, up hills and stairs, soaked from head to toe by the time I reached the building. By the time I made it inside, I felt completely drained.

Still, I was hopeful.

I told the concierge I was visiting family. He asked, "Are they expecting you?" I said no. Then he picked up the phone and called the unit. "You have a guest here. He says he's family." The concierge turned to me and said one of the most devastating things I have ever heard in my life. Essentially, they denied knowing me and expressed to the concierge they weren't receiving any guests. At that moment, something inside me broke. I had not just been turned away from a building. I had been turned away by someone I loved. I stood there, soaked, exhausted, and stunned, trying to make sense of what had just happened.

I left a note before I walked back into the night. I never received a response. The rain had stopped by the time I reached the train, but the weight I carried with me did not. I remember sitting alone, feeling a deep ache settle in my chest and stomach at the same time. It was the kind of pain that does not rush. It sits with you.

What hurt the most was not the rejection itself. It was what it represented. I had always hoped for closeness, for connection, for a family that stayed together. That night forced me to face the reality that some of those hopes might never look the way I imagined. For a long time, I did not know what to do with that pain. I only knew it was real and it was deep. That experience hurt more than losing the game ever did. Not all pain looks the same, but ignoring it always leads to the same place.

THE PAIN BEHIND THE PAIN

When sports ends, most people assume the pain comes from losing the game itself. The practices, the competition, the dream, and while that loss is real, it is often not the whole story. For many athletes, the end of sports doesn't just hurt because something ended. It hurts because something underneath gets exposed.

This is why the pain of transition often feels bigger than expected. You are not just grieving what you lost. You are being confronted with things you learned to carry long before the final whistle ever blew. You are being invited to deal with what was already there.

For some, it is rejection, being overlooked, being cut, or being told you were not enough. For others, it is betrayal, broken trust, abandoned relationships or people who were supposed to protect you, but did not. For many, it is pain that goes all the way back to childhood. Moments where you learned to perform, achieve, or compete in order to feel valued. The game gave you something to hide behind. It gave you a place where effort was rewarded and identity felt clear.

Former NBA player Dwyane Wade once said, *"The biggest thing I've learned is that your scars don't go away when the lights turn off."* For athletes, the lights turning off often happens when the game ends and that is when unresolved pain starts asking to be addressed. This does not mean sports caused the pain, it means sports helped manage it for a while.

That is why rejection can feel louder without the uniform. Why criticism cuts deeper. Why silence feels heavier than it should. You are not just reacting to what is happening now. You are reacting to what it reminds you of and until you recognize that, it is easy to think something is wrong with you. You may judge yourself like, "I'm too sensitive" or "I'm being weak." That's not the case; your pain is just being exposed.

WHAT HAPPENS WHEN YOU DON'T LET GO

Every athlete knows this is true: you can skip reps in practice, avoid the weight room, even rush through film and half-listen to coaching, but when the lights come on and the game starts, everything you avoided has a way of showing itself. Life is no different. If you hold onto bitterness, resentment, or disappointment from the past, especially around how your sports career ended, it eventually begins to shape how you move through life. Not because you want it to, but because unprocessed pain always finds a way to express itself. Often it leaks into our relationships, how we show up at work, and navigate every day tasks.

For some people, it shows up as defensiveness. Every comment feels like an attack. Even helpful feedback feels personal. You feel the need to explain yourself, protect yourself, or push back, even when you know you might be wrong. It becomes exhausting, both for you and for the people around you.

For others, it shows up as insecurity. Deep down, you are unsure of your worth, so you assume others are questioning it too. You secretly don't think you're good enough, so you transfer this onto others and assume they don't think you're good enough either. As a result, you always feel that you have something to prove. You struggle to relax and simply be yourself because you are constantly trying to measure up.

Unresolved pain can also show up as trust issues. You stay guarded. You assume people have hidden motives. Instead of giving others the benefit of the doubt, you brace for disappointment. You tell yourself you are being careful, but over time, that posture turns into isolation.

Sometimes, it shows up as pessimism. You expect things to go wrong. You focus on what will not work instead of what could. You become critical or cynical, not because you enjoy it, but because disappointment feels safer than hope. Inspiring speaker, Benjamin Zander, described a cynic as "a passionate person who doesn't want to be disappointed again." There's even a scripture that says "hope deferred makes the heart sick." Meaning disappointed hits deep.

All of this points to the same truth; pain has a way of shaping us. When pain goes unchecked, it affects every area of your life. Relationships become strained. Opportunities become limited. Trust becomes harder to build. People begin to keep their distance, not because they do not care, but because pain has a way of making connection difficult. You can work hard to hide it, but eventually it leaks out. And unless you are willing to let go of what hurt you, you risk allowing the past to keep deciding who you become next.

The good news is this does not have to be your story. Letting go does not mean pretending the pain didn't matter. It means deciding it will not control Lewis Smedes, a renowned Christian theologian from Fuller Seminary once said, "To forgive is to set a prisoner free and discover that the prisoner was you." Many people wonder why moving on is so difficult because they are being held hostage by bitterness, unforgiveness, anger, and sadness.

LETTING GO CREATES LEVERAGE

One of the most important lessons I've learned about moving forward is this: letting go is not about pretending something didn't hurt. It's about deciding what that hurt is going to produce in your life. For a long time, I misunderstood what letting go meant. I thought it required forgetting. I thought it meant minimizing what happened or acting as if it didn't matter. However, real letting go is not denial, it's direction. It's choosing not to let a painful moment continue shaping your identity long after the moment has passed.

When I think back to the experience I shared earlier I can see how the rejection I experienced marked something significant. At the time, all I felt was hurt, but over time, through conversations with people I trusted and honest reflection, I began to see what that pain revealed. It showed me how deeply I value connection. It exposed how much I care about unity, restoration, and people feeling seen. What once felt like pure loss eventually became clarity.

That shift did not happen overnight. I had to make a decision. I could either let that experience harden me, or I could let it shape me. I could carry resentment forward and allow it to influence how I approached every relationship afterward, or I could release it and ask a better question: What can this teach me? That question changed everything because I chose to let go of the bitterness attached to that experience, I was able to learn from it instead of living inside it. The pain didn't disappear, but it stopped controlling me and in time, it began to inform the work I do today. I now spend my life helping people navigate transitions, find direction, and connect to opportunities. The very thing that once felt like rejection helped clarify what I was built to contribute.

That is what letting go creates. It creates leverage. Leverage is the ability to use something difficult as momentum instead of weight. When you refuse to let go, pain sits on your shoulders. When you release it, pain moves behind you and begins pushing you forward. The same experience can either drain you or direct you. The difference is not in what happened. The difference is in what you choose to do with it.

Every person will experience disappointment. Every athlete will experience loss. Some wounds will come from the game. Others will come from life. But none of them are meant to be wasted. When you hold onto anger, it spreads. When you choose to forgive, it clears space. And only in that space can growth happen.

Letting go is not weakness, it is taking leadership over your own future. It is the decision to stop allowing yesterday to dictate tomorrow. Without that decision, no amount of talent, ambition, or effort will move you where you want to go. Your pain has potential, but it only becomes power when you are willing to release it and learn from it.

HOW TO LET IT GO

Letting go is not a single emotional moment. It is a process, and like anything meaningful, it requires intention.

1. Bring What You've Buried to the Surface

You cannot release what you refuse to acknowledge. The first step in letting go is admitting that something still hurts. Not the surface-level version of the story. Not the cleaned-up summary you tell people. The real version, the part that still stings when you think about it.

Most of us are comfortable admitting the "acceptable" emotions, frustration, disappointment, maybe even anger. But there are other emotions we tend to bury because they make us feel exposed, rejection, shame, betrayal, insecurity. Those are harder to name. They require vulnerability. They require honesty.

Letting go begins when you stop pretending those feelings are not there. For some people, especially those who have experienced deeper trauma, this work should not be done alone. A trained counselor, therapist, pastor, or trusted mentor can help you process what surfaces. There is strength in seeking help. When you open wounds that have been closed for years, you want support in handling them well.

A practical starting point is simple but powerful. Take a moment try this: Write down the most painful or disappointing moments from your past. Next to each one, write the emotions you still carry because of it. Be honest. Do not just list what happened; name how it affected you. Then write the names of the people involved and make a decision.

Forgiveness is not pretending it did not matter. It is saying, "It mattered. It hurt, but I will not let it or them control me anymore."

Next, speak that decision out loud. There is something powerful about hearing yourself choose freedom. It could sound something like this:

"You hurt me, and I still feel the pain. I know that if you had known how much what you did would hurt me, you would not have done what you did. I have also hurt other people in the past, so I know what it's like to hurt people without meaning to. God freely gives me grace and forgiveness when I don't deserve it. Sometimes, I even do the wrong thing on purpose, and He still gives me grace and forgives me. We are all flawed and need to have grace extended to us when we hurt each other. In the same way that I would hope others would forgive me, even when I don't de-

serve it, I extend that same grace to you. I forgive you."

You may feel grief. You may feel anger. You may feel relief. Let yourself feel it. Emotions are not permanent; they move when you allow them to.

2. Find Healthy Ways to Release

Once you have brought the pain to the surface, you need somewhere for it to go. Keeping it inside only pushes it deeper. Giving it voice begins to release it. Talking to someone you trust, someone who will listen without judgment, can change everything. Sometimes clarity comes simply from hearing your own words out loud.

For athletes especially, physical movement can also be a powerful outlet. You spent years releasing stress through competition and training. When that stops, the release often stops too. Keep moving. Run. Lift. Box. Train. Sweat. Move your body with intention. Physical movement has a way of loosening what feels stuck emotionally. When the body moves, the mind and heart often follow.

After sports ends, you no longer have structured outlets built into your weeks, so you have to choose them. Do not let yourself become stagnant. Movement creates momentum.

3. Re-Imagine the Purpose of Your Pain

Perspective changes everything. If you see every painful experience as something that ruined you, you will carry it like damage. But if you begin to ask what it taught you, what it built in you, or what it revealed about you, your view starts to shift.

Pain can develop depth. It can build empathy. , strengthen character, clarify what matters most. That does not mean what happened was good. It means something good can come from it.

You can choose to see your past as a series of setbacks, or you can see it as preparation. You can frame it as destruction, or you can see it as development.

Often, the very experiences that felt like they were breaking you were shaping you. They forced growth. They exposed weaknesses. They built resilience and prepared you for leadership in ways comfort never could.

When you begin to look at your pain through that lens, it no longer feels random. It becomes formative. When pain becomes formative, it becomes leverage.

RUN THIS PLAY

Letting go is not a concept. It is a decision, and decisions require action. This week, don't just think about what you've read. Practice it.

1. IDENTIFY WHAT YOU'RE STILL CARRYING

When reading the quote mentioned earlier that says ,"forgiveness sets the prisoner free, only to realize the prisoner was you.", who comes to mind when you read that?

Write their name down. Do not overthink it. The first name that surfaces usually tells you something. Then ask yourself an honest question: What am I still holding against this person? Be specific. Is it anger? Disappointment? Embarrassment? Betrayal?

You do not have to call them immediately, but you do have to acknowledge what you are carrying. Clarity is the first step toward freedom.

2. HAVE THE CONVERSATION, IF IT'S SAFE AND WISE

If it is appropriate and safe to do so, consider having a conversation with the person involved. Not to attack. Not to win. Not to relive the argument. But to release what you've been holding.

Adapted from *The Art of Feeding Heroes* by Jean Marie Jobs, here is a simple structure to guide you:

- Share what you have been carrying. Be specific.

- Acknowledge where you may have made assumptions or filled in gaps.

- State clearly that you are choosing to release it.

- Invite them to share what they heard and how they experienced the situation.

- Listen without interrupting or defending.

- Stay present, even if it feels uncomfortable.

Not every situation will allow for a conversation. In those cases, forgiveness can still happen internally. Releasing someone does not always require their participation.

3. CREATE A DAILY REMINDER OF YOUR DECISION

Forgiveness is rarely a one-time emotional release. It is often a repeated choice.

For the next 21 days, remind yourself daily that you are not carrying that weight anymore. You can look in the mirror if that helps. You can say it out loud. You can write it in a journal.

Say something simple and direct, like: *"I choose to release what hurt me. I refuse to let it control my future."*

If faith is central to your life, you can anchor that decision in your belief in grace and forgiveness. If not, anchor it in your commitment to your own growth. The goal is the same. Freedom.

4. PAY ATTENTION TO WHAT SHIFTS

Throughout the week, notice how you respond in situations that would normally trigger you. Are you less reactive? More at peace? Still tense?

Write down what changes. Even small shifts matter.

Letting go creates leverage, but only if you follow through.

PLAY #3:
DEVELOP YOUR IDENTITY

The game taught us discipline, taught us teamwork, taught us to push our limits, and it taught us how to perform. We knew when the whistle blew, when the lights turned on, it was game time and the only thing that mattered was how well we did on the field or court. If we're honest, I think most athletes would admit that their performance was deeply connected to their identity. Think about it, "oh, he's so fast, she's the best on the team.." and so on. Which begs the question, who are we when we're not performing?

I WAS STILL PERFORMING.

When football ended, I didn't have a plan because football was my plan. My identity was so wrapped in the game and who I thought I'd be with it, I didn't consider anything else. I simply did what I thought I was supposed to do or at least pretended like it.

At this point, I was in my mid-20's working several jobs. I did everything from working for my father's chiropractic office and a network marketing company, to working on campus at APU and doing gig work like Uber Eats, Door Dash, and other various contracted tasks. While I was always busy, I didn't feel like I was actually going anywhere or doing anything important.

I've always struggled with wanting to look good for other people and this season only heightened it. I had a deep need to be seen as productive and successful, especially since my football career had come to an end. To keep up this facade, I would get dressed up: blazer, button down, jeans, and dress shoes, and go to Starbucks. I would set up a little work station with my computer and two phones so people would not just think I was doing something, but that I was important. I exchanged the field and jersey for dress clothes and busy work. I was still looking for claps and accolades, it just looked different. I still wanted people to say things like, "oh look at him, he's doing so good."

Maybe you can relate. Not with the dressing up and going to Starbucks part, but maybe trying to keep up a facade. Trying to figure out what to do to prove your value, that you're still accomplishing something. Performance can be a trap. What no one really teaches us is how to step out of it. For many of us, the trap runs deeper than we realize.

THE PERFORMANCE TRAP

I didn't realize how deep my need to perform ran until I was sitting in a room listening to a woman challenge everything I thought I knew about identity. During my time in grad school at APU, I attended a four-day transformational leadership training. I signed up because I wanted to grow, but I had no idea how much it would expose. The facilitator was Jean Marie Jobs, who later became a mentor of mine. On the last day, she introduced a concept that stopped me in my tracks.

She called it the Be, Do, Have cycle. She explained that most people live in reverse order. We think if we do enough and have enough, then we will finally be enough.

If I do well,

If I have success,

Then I'll be confident.

If I do what's impressive,

If I have the title, the platform, the recognition,

Then I'll be secure.

As she spoke, I felt exposed because that was me. Football had trained me to live in that cycle without realizing it. Perform well and you earn your spot. Win games and you earn respect. Hit certain marks and you earn attention. It's not malicious; it's just how the system works. Over time, though, that pattern can shape how you see yourself.

Without knowing it, I had built my identity on performance and when performance became uncertain, so did I. That Starbucks season wasn't random. It was the cycle playing out in real time. I thought if I could do something that looked productive, and if I could have the appearance of importance, then I would finally feel secure again.

But it never lasted, because identity does not work that way. We were not created to *do* in order to become someone. We were created to be first. Scripture says we are "God's workmanship, created for good works" (Ephesians 2:10). Notice the order. We are created first. The works come from that place.

Many people quote Psalm 139, "We are fearfully and wonderfully made," without processing how that speaks to identity before achievement.

When you understand who you are, your doing changes. You stop performing to prove something and you start acting from conviction and authenticity. One of the things I've heard Myron Golden teach is that success flows from identity. You do not build your "being" from what you achieve; you build your achievements from who you have decided to become. That shift changes everything.

When you live from Be, Do, Have, instead of Do, Have, Be, you start from identity from purpose and your values. Then your actions flow from that foundation and over time, the results follow.

Now let's be honest, it may be easy to understand the cycle in theory. It's harder to admit how easily we fall into it. The performance is tempting. We live in a culture that constantly reinforces it. Work harder. Earn more. Build more. Post more. Achieve more. We're told that if we just reach the next level, the next title, the next milestone, then we'll finally feel secure.

But think about it.

You wanted the better-paying job. You got it. Did that settle everything inside you? You wanted the newer car. You got it. Did that bring lasting peace? You wanted the relationship. You got it. Are you completely fulfilled?

The answers vary, but the pattern doesn't. We keep believing that the next thing will complete us. Athletes feel this deeply because the system reinforces it. Score ten touchdowns, and you start thinking about twelve. Have a great season, and you wonder what it would look like to have an even better one. There's nothing wrong with setting goals. Growth is healthy. But when you believe that "just one more" will finally make you feel secure, the pursuit never ends.

I've seen it on the court. A player so focused on getting his numbers up that he stops passing. Every possession becomes personal. Not because he hates his teammates, but because he believes his future depends on those stats. In his mind, if he takes all the shots, he'll have all the points. If he has all the points, he'll be the star. If he's the star, he'll get the offer. If he gets the offer, then he'll finally be somebody.

That's the cycle. If we're honest, it doesn't stop when the season ends. It just changes uniforms. We trade jerseys for job titles.

I remember working in Christian ministry in the APU campus pastor's office and being overly focused on projects and events. I was so focused on doing things for God that I missed out on spending time with Him. I put enormous amounts of energy into every event, but it was not really with a focus on serving God. Instead, I did it to look good to others and gain recognition from them for my efforts. It was my own Do-Have-Be cycle. I thought that if I did a lot of events and things that kept me busy for God, I would have an honorable relationship with God and I would be fulfilled. But instead, all of the work and non-stop activity just led to me feeling tired and depleted. I was so busy that I wasn't having the communal time with God that I needed to just sit with Him, be his son and be loved and accepted by Him. All of the performance and busyness led to me feeling like I had just checked all the boxes, but had I actually gotten to do what really mattered?

At the end of the day, I felt tired, spun out and physically exhausted. It took some time for me to learn that my performance is not what gave me value. Who I am when I'm being authentically me, even if I'm doing nothing at all, is enough to give my life value, because I belong to God. If He calls me valuable, which He does, what others say really doesn't matter. What I do is no longer correlated with my worth.

You were created with inherent worth. That's your starting point. You were also created with the power to choose. Maybe you're thinking, " *Okay, I see the cycle. I've fallen into the trap more than once. So now what?*" It's simple, you get to decide

You get to choose the kind of person you will be. You get to develop character, define your values, and build conviction. You're born with purpose, that doesn't change. But identity? Identity is something you shape. The game may have influenced you in one season of life, but it does not get to define you for the rest of it.

So the real question becomes this: If you are not your performance, then who are you becoming? And more importantly, how do you build that intentionally?

HOW TO DEVELOP YOUR IDENTITY

If identity is something you shape, then you cannot shape it accidentally.It requires attention.

1. START WITH HONEST SELF-EVALUATION

If you are going to build an identity beyond sports, you have to begin by getting to know yourself without the uniform.

This is where most people rush. They want to declare who they are becoming without first understanding who they actually are. Slow down.

Ask yourself questions you may not have paused long enough to consider:

- What do I truly value?
- What qualities define me when no one is watching?
- What energizes me?
- What frustrates me?

- What do people consistently notice about me?
- What parts of myself am I proud of?
- What parts of myself still need work?

This is not about creating a version of yourself that sounds impressive, but about uncovering what is already there. You cannot build an authentic identity on a false foundation.

2. ACCEPT WHAT IS ALREADY THERE

When I say you get to choose your identity, I'm not saying you get to pretend parts of you don't exist.You don't build identity from scratch. You build it from raw material. Some of that raw material is beautiful. Some of it feels complicated. Some of it comes from experiences you'd rather not revisit, but all of it shaped you.

Before you decide who you're becoming, you have to be willing to look honestly at who you already are.

There may be traits about you that you've tried to hide. There may be parts of your story you've minimize or moments in your past that still carry weight.

Ignoring them doesn't make them disappear. It just leaves them undefined. I had to learn this through something simple: my name.

My full name is Adedeji Olajide. I come from a Nigerian family, and in our culture, names carry meaning. They reflect heritage, story, and identity. When I was younger, I felt embarrassed by my name because it sounded different. It was long. It stood out and all I wanted was to blend in. So I shortened it. I chose Deji because it felt more comfortable, but as I grew, I began to see my name differently. It represented my family. My history. My roots. I noticed when I started saying it confidently, I wasn't just introducing myself. I was owning where I came from and people responded to that.

The meaning of my name is "double crown." So, to remind myself never to settle and always be bold about who I am, I often use the 2 golden crown emojis as a signature on social media and text messages. I also decided to name my consulting business Double Krown Consulting Inc. as a reminder to be who I am in the marketplace.

Nothing about my name changed. What changed was my acceptance of it.There are parts of you that function the same way. Maybe it's your name, your background, your personality or maybe it's something you experienced that shaped how you see the world. You don't have to glorify every painful thing that happened, but you also don't have to pretend it didn't shape you.

You wouldn't be you without it. Identity development doesn't mean erasing your story. It means becoming curious about it and asking, "How has this shaped me? What strength came from this? What perspective did this give me?"

You get to choose who you become, but you do that by building on what's already there, not by dismissing it.

3. ASK THE CREATOR

There's a principle that says when the purpose of a thing is not known, abuse is inevitable. If you don't understand what something was designed for, you will eventually misuse it. Not intentionally, just ignorantly.

You wouldn't buy a complex piece of equipment and guess your way through it. You would look for the manual. You would consult the designer. You would try to understand its intended function before pushing it to its limits. The same applies to us.

If you don't understand what you were created for, you will default to what the culture tells you you're for. Things like, achievement, performance, attention, income, and status. When those things become your purpose, they start to misuse you.

You were not designed to be consumed by applause or live in comparison and you were certainly not designed to earn your worth. For me, this realization brought me back to God.

Scripture says we are created intentionally, that we are known before we are seen, that we are formed with care. When I began to view myself through that lens, identity shifted. It became less about proving something and more about aligning with something.

You may be strong in your faith. You may be questioning it. You may not claim one at all. Wherever you stand, consider this: you did not design yourself. There is intention behind your existence and when you seek clarity from the One who designed you, identity stops being something you chase and becomes something you uncover and cultivate.

RUN THIS PLAY

Set aside 10–15 uninterrupted minutes this week and work through the following.

1. STRIP THE LABELS

In your journal, answer this question honestly: If you removed your job, your sport, your accolades, your résumé, and your achievements... who are you?

2. REMOVE COMPARISON

Now consider this: What would it look like to fully live out your vision without comparing your life to anyone else's?

How would you move differently?

What would you stop chasing?

What would you finally give yourself permission to pursue?

3. PRACTICE SELF-ACCEPTANCE

Find a quiet moment. Stand in front of a mirror. Look at yourself without adjusting anything. No fixing. No critiquing. No mental editing.

Just observe.

Notice how quickly your mind wants to judge or improve something. Let that pass and stay present.

When you feel grounded, say out loud:

"I accept you."

When you reach a point of being comfortable gazing at yourself and accepting that who you're looking at is who you are, say to yourself, "I love you.

I challenge you to do this anytime you look in the mirror.

4. SEEK HONEST FEEDBACK

Ask someone who knows you well a simple question:"How do you experience me?" Follow it with: "What do you think I'm naturally good at?" "What stands out about me?"

5. TRY THESE AFFIRMATION

For the next 21 days, repeat this daily: "I am loved. I am accepted. I belong."

Feel free to draft your own or find others to add.

PLAY #4:
TRY SOMETHING NEW

I wish I could tell you that my transition from college football into the next phase of life was clean and predictable. It wasn't. It didn't look like one clear path unfolding in front of me. It looked more like stepping stones, one opportunity after another. Most often, they were unexpected and none of them felt like "the plan."

Three years after football ended, I was in a Master of Divinity program at APU. I was working part-time as a graduate assistant. That role exposed me to student development, spiritual formation, and the behind-the-scenes work of running a campus ministry serving thousands of students. I learned how to build programs, structure teams, organize retreats, lead small groups, plan chapel services, and develop strategy. At the time, I thought I was just doing a job, but, looking back, I was building muscles I didn't know I would need.

Around that same season, I went on a mission trip to Mexico. It was definitely a new kind of experience for me. We slept in tents at a local campground, and every day, we had live worship and community time. In addition to visiting a local orphanage, part of our assignment included serving inside a local prison every day. During our visits we did things like play basketball, soccer, and dominoes with the inmates. We made lunch for them, listened to their stories, and shared some of our own as well.

What stands out to me now is not just the trip, but what happened before it. I almost didn't go. I had already decided in my mind that I wouldn't be able to raise the money. I assumed people wouldn't support it. I was defeated before I even started, but when I committed to going anyway, resources began to show up, donations came in, supplies were given and support arrived from unexpected places. That trip taught me something I could not have learned on a football field: when you attach yourself to something bigger than yourself, provision often follows purpose.

As I kept saying yes to new environments, something interesting happened. Leaders began approaching me with opportunities. Job offers surfaced. One role paid double what I was making. A new apartment opened up near campus and furniture was even donated. Doors that I didn't even know existed began to open.

None of this would have happened if I had stayed still. Every new opportunity added something: skills, perspective, confidence, and connection. I did not realize it at the time, but I was assembling pieces of a future I could not yet see.

REPS BEYOND THE GAME

That's the part many athletes miss. You don't find the next version of yourself by sitting on the bench of uncertainty. You find it by getting back in motion. There is a line often attributed to Mark Twain: "Twenty years from now you will be more disappointed by the things you didn't do than by the ones you did." What he understood is this: regret rarely comes from trying, it comes from staying still.

You did not become who you were on the field by waiting until you felt ready. You became that player through repetition. Through uncomfortable reps, drills that did not always feel productive in the moment, but built something underneath the surface.

Life after sports works the same way. If identity is something you shape, then shaping requires experimentation. It requires the humility to be new at something again, to be average again and risk looking inexperienced after years of being skilled. This can be uncomfortable, but it's necessary.

Discovering your purpose and developing identity comes through stepping into new environments and paying attention to what happens inside you.

What energizes you?

What drains you?

What feels natural?

What feels forced?

These are reps beyond the game. Every internship, side project, conversation, risk you take, and small "yes" to something unfamiliar matters. They are all building awareness. Some of those reps will sharpen your skills while others will clarify your values. Both are necessary.

When you're not willing to engage these kinds of reps, transition becomes all the more difficult. You don't just miss opportunities, you miss self-discovery. You never learn what else you're capable of or test hidden strengths. You never stretch beyond the identity you once held and without that stretching, it becomes harder to imagine who you could become next.

There was another layer to this season for me. While I was stepping into new professional environments, I was also doing internal work. I started reading more. Listening to teaching that challenged my thinking. Practicing affirmations. Paying attention to my thoughts instead of letting them run unchecked. I trained my body daily, even though I was no longer competing. I ran. I lifted. I watched what I ate. I surrounded myself with driven, focused people who stretched me intellectually and spiritually.

On paper, I was still living at home and making very little money. Internally, I felt rich, sharp, focused, and like I was expanding. That internal shift mattered more than any job title I held during that season because trying new things externally while neglecting growth internally would have left me scattered. Personal development gave structure to the experimentation. It accelerated everything.

HOW TO TRY NEW EXPERIENCES

This season is not about having all the answers. It's about being willing to try. My willingness to try is what gave me many of the lessons I'm sharing in this book.

1. GET A COACH

Every serious athlete understands this: no one reaches their potential alone. On the field, you had coaches who saw what you couldn't see. They corrected your form, challenged your habits, and called out blind spots. They pushed you beyond what you would have pushed yourself. Why would life after sports be any different?

If you're struggling to identify which opportunities are worth pursuing, or you feel unsure about how your strengths translate beyond the game, get guidance. This could be a career coach, life coach, mentor, or university career center. Having someone trained to assess your skills, personality, and interests and help you test them in real environments.

A good coach doesn't hand you a script for your life. They help you see yourself more clearly. They ask better questions. They point you toward rooms you might not have considered walking into on your own.

Some of the experiences you try will fit, others won't, and thats ok. The goal isn't perfection, it's progress. Sometimes the fastest way forward is having someone in your corner who can see the field from a different angle.

2. PUT SKIN IN THE GAME

I like to say, "Pay the cost to be the boss." In other words, invest in where you're trying to go. In sports, this wasn't up for debate. You paid in sweat, in early mornings and late nights, and in soreness. You understood that development was not free.

If you are serious about discovering what's next, you have to invest in your own expansion. That may mean paying for a workshop, enrolling in a certification program, attending a conference, or joining a training environment that stretches you. These opportunities are rarely free, but neither is progress.

Jim Rohn once said, "Formal education will make you a living; self-education will make you a fortune."

There is wisdom in that. When you choose to invest in your growth, even when money feels tight, you send a message to yourself: *I am worth developing.* When you've put something on the line, you show up differently, prepare more intentionally and engage more closely.

Investment isn't only internal, your presentation matters too. You may no longer wear a jersey, but you are still representing something. I want to challenge you to upgrade your wardrobe. Purchase a few well-chosen pieces that communicate readiness and professionalism. This can shift how you carry yourself and how others receive you. When your internal commitment and your external preparation match, opportunities recognize you faster.

3. DIVERSIFY YOUR EXPERIENCES

If you look at my transition season on paper, it might seem scattered; ministry work, fundraising, graduate school, leadership roles, travel, new environments, and new responsibilities.

Diversifying my experiences diversified me. Each environment sharpened something different: communication skills, leadership, organization, resilience, and discernment. Some opportunities confirmed what I enjoyed and others clarified what I did not. Both were equally valuable. None of those experiences guaranteed success. I could have failed in any one of them. That risk was real, but the greater risk would have been staying comfortable and learning nothing.

You cannot let the possibility of failure keep you from stepping into something new. Growth rarely happens inside environments you've already mastered. It happens when you enter rooms where you don't have a reference point, where you're not the expert, and you're now learning in real time.

John Maxwell says, "Sometimes you win, sometimes you learn." That mindset changes everything. When learning becomes the goal, fear loses its power. Be willing to try experiences that feel unfamiliar, even ones where you have no prior training or advantage. You may discover that what you never considered before may quietly reveal itself as something you were built for.

RUN THIS PLAY

Set aside 10–15 uninterrupted minutes this week and work through the following

JOURNAL PROMPTS

1. If money and time were not limitations, how would you spend your life?

2. What experiences have you secretly wanted to try but never allowed yourself to explore because of sports, expectations, or fear? List them. Big or small. Professional or personal.

3. Where in the world would you love to spend time, and why? What about that place pulls you? What would you do there? What version of you feels alive in that environment?

ACTION STEPS

Commit to taking the following actions this week. After you have completed each action, write a few notes to remind yourself about the details of what you did, how it felt, and what additional follow-up needs to be done.

- Based on the information learned in this chapter, commit to one action step of your choice.

Make sure the action has a clear outcome/result and has a date by which you will complete it.

- Communicate with one person and let them know what you will be doing so they can keep you accountable on the day the action is to be completed.

AFFIRMATION

Repeat this affirmation (while looking at yourself in the mirror) every day for the next 21 days:

"Today will be filled with unexpected opportunities. I have an abundance of energy. Amazing people are always around me, and I always meet great friends."

PLAY #5:
DON'T LOSE YOUR EDGE

Being an athlete gave you something most people spend years trying to build, an edge. Not just physical ability or talent, but an internal edge. The kind forged in early mornings, disciplined routines, film study, structured schedules, and periods of conditioning like Hell Week.

I can remember it like it was yesterday: the first day of fall camp. The entire team packed into the meeting room. It was close to 10 p.m., but no one looked tired. Coach Victor Santa Cruz stood at the front, walking us through the schedule for the next day. Phones were out because everyone wanted to be ready to capture it.

For two straight weeks, there was no guessing about what the day required. No drifting. No wasted hours. You woke up with purpose, moved with intention, and went to bed knowing you had emptied the tank. It was grueling, but also rewarding and incredibly valuable..

Hell Week was never just about football. It was about capacity. If you had to endure anything like this then you'd agree it taught you how to function when tired. How to execute when uncomfortable. How to stay disciplined when motivation faded. It built grit, focus, and resilience into your nervous system.

As you transition into this new season and begin making new plays, what was built in you as an athlete is still valuable, I would even argue, necessary.

USE IT OR LOSE IT

I'm sure you've heard the phrase "use it or lose it" before. Think about that foreign language you studied years ago. At one point, you could form sentences, understood basic conversation. Maybe you even passed the class with a decent grade, but what happened when you stopped speaking it? It faded.

If you do not intentionally apply the survival skills and success characteristics you developed as an athlete, they will fade in the same way. The discipline that took years to build. The structured thinking, mental toughness, and the ability to execute when you don't feel like it. If you don't translate them into your professional life, your business, your relationships, your calling – they atrophy.

Here's the part most people don't want to hear: once they fade, they are much harder to recapture. Rebuilding discipline is far more difficult than maintaining it. It's like trying to recover a language you once spoke fluently; possible, but painfully slow.

HOW TO KEEP YOUR EDGE:

David Goggins is known for what he calls the "40 Percent Rule." He says, "When your mind is telling you that you're done, you're only at 40% of what you're truly capable of." Even research confirms you still have fuel and energy to expend although you feel like you're at your quitting point.

The way you keep your edge is the same way you built it: you continue to train. You continue to apply the disciplines, build structure, focus, and standards for yourself, even when no one else is. No one is going to make you wake up early and build a routine for you. This season requires self leadership and that means choosing to operate at the level you know you're capable of. Doing what's necessary, not just comfortable or your preference. You can start here:

1. KEEP A VISIBLE CALENDAR.

For most of your athletic career, however long it lasted, your life revolved around a schedule. Practices during the week. Games on weekends. Tournaments, lifts, time to study film, academic classes, team meetings, family, travel, recovery, and the list goes on.

If you were anything like me, you had your season mapped out months in advance. All the key dates were marked on a calendar before the year even started. In my mind, there is no such thing as an athlete who has not had to master living by a schedule. In a world where many people are scattered, reactive, and constantly claiming they do not have enough time, you already understand how to organize your day and execute within a plan. That's part of your edge, use it.

Apply that same discipline to this season of your life by creating a visible calendar. Not tasks buried in the notes app on your phone that you rarely check, but something you see every day. Try planning at least one quarter at a time. Block out work commitments, growth opportunities, family time, church or ministry responsibilities, personal development, and rest. Be as specific and detailed as you can. Then place that calendar somewhere visible like your workspace, mirror, or on your wall. Allow this calendar to be the anchor for your discipline, focus and momentum on a daily basis.

2. SET GOALS FOR YOURSELF.

Michael Jordan once said, "You have to expect things of yourself before you can do them." That is goal setting in its simplest form. Expectation precedes achievement.

As an athlete, you lived by it. You had both individual goals and team goals. You trained with outcomes in mind. Goals reminded you where you were headed and they stretched you beyond what felt comfortable.

This can be translated to your next play. Set goals for your personal growth, your finances, career aspiration, business development, and your impact. Do not drift into this season without targets.

There are countless models for goal setting, but beneath every method, the principle remains the same. Your goals should be specific and measurable. Edwin Locke, a leading goal setting theorist said, "specific and challenging goals lead to higher performance than vague or easy goals." If your goals do not demand growth, they will not produce it. The objective is not to set goals that feel achievable. It is to set goals that require you to become more disciplined, more focused, and more capable than you are today.

The same muscle that pushed you toward championships can push you toward excellence in this season.

3. MAINTAIN YOUR MOMENTUM.

The longer the gap between the discipline you lived in as an athlete and the discipline you apply in this season, the harder it becomes to reengage it. Do not give yourself an extended break or wait for the "right time." Also don't assume you can pause the skills you developed in sports and easily turn them back on later.

In physics, an object in motion stays in motion, and an object at rest stays at rest unless acted upon by force. Momentum matters, use it to your advantage.

If you keep moving, even at a different pace, you preserve your edge. If you drift for too long, rebuilding will require far more effort than maintaining rhythm. You know this from training. The first workout after time off is always harder than the last one before the break.

Do not make this season harder than it needs to be. You already bring a strong set of skills and discipline that can carry over to your next play.

RUN THIS PLAY

Start applying your athletic experiences to your next phase in life by writing about the following in your journal for the next 10 – 15 minutes:

- Write down 5 success principles that your sport taught you.
- In what ways can you carry these principles over to your career and life after sports?
- What is the hardest lesson in sports you learned that you are now really grateful for, and why?

ACTION STEPS:

Commit to taking the following actions this week. After you have completed each action, write a few notes to remind yourself about the details of what you did, how it felt, and what additional follow-up needs to be done.

- Purchase a visible 36 x 54 12-month calendar and place it on your wall.
- On the calendar, write at least one goal for the year in each of these categories: Health, Finances, Relationships, Career, Spiritual.

AFFIRMATION

For the next 21 days, stand in front of the mirror and speak your future out loud.

Use one of your goals to create a personal affirmation. Make it clear, specific, and bold.

Speak it in the present tense, as if you are already living it. Not because you are pretending, but because you are training your mind to align with where you are going.

Use this example as a guide:

"I am a wildly successful coach who earns $8,400 a month, and I feel fully alive in my calling." Here's another, *"I am disciplined. I am focused. I apply my edge daily, and I create results that reflect my full potential."*

Now write your own.

BECOME A "SUPER CONNECTOR"

One of the most overlooked skills you developed as an athlete had nothing to do with strength or speed. It was relational. You learned how to function inside a team. You learned how to read people, communicate under pressure, adjust your role when necessary, and collaborate toward a shared outcome. Championships are never won alone. You may have had individual stats, but the scoreboard always reflected collective effort.

That doesn't change when you're no longer on a team. In fact, in the next season of your life, it becomes even more valuable. Success beyond sports is rarely about raw talent. It is about relationships because doors open through people. Opportunities travel through networks and influence often expands through collaboration. The same instinct that helped you understand your teammate's tendencies, antici-pate movement, and respond in real time is the same instinct that can position you strategically in business, ministry, leadership, or entrepreneurship.

CONNECTION BIGGER THAN JUST THE BURRITO

Since I was a young kid, I can remember being com-fortable starting conversations and keeping them going. By age sixteen, I would find myself talking to elderly people, principals, janitors, store clerks, and even babies without hesitation. I did not have lan-guage for it then, but looking back, I recognize that I was naturally wired to connect. God had given me a kind of relational confidence that made interaction feel easy.

A few years ago, I was at one of my favorite Mex-ican restaurants in Corona, California, Miguel's Jr. I had recently started eating a plant-based diet and ordered a burrito with no meat, no sour cream, and light cheese. It was terrible. When the server brought it out, it was covered in sour cream. I polite-ly asked if they could remake it without the sour cream, and they did.

What stayed with me wasn't the mistake itself, but the reaction. The server was sincerely apologetic, saying, "Oh my gosh, I'm so sorry. Will you forgive me? Are you going to be mad at me now" I had only met him once before, but during that visit we had exchanged conversation beyond the transaction. In that moment, it was clear that the error meant more to him than a misplaced ingredient. It was not just about the burrito. He felt like he had missed an opportunity to listen well and to serve me properly. That is the power of connection.

When you build genuine relational equity, ordinary interactions carry more weight. People remember you, they feel seen, they feel heard and that changes how they respond to you in future moments.

THE POWER OF LISTENING.

In *Caring Enough to Hear and Be Heard*, David W. Augsburger writes: "Being heard is so close to being loved that for the average person, they are almost indistinguishable." Sit with that.

To be heard is to feel valued and to be listened to is to feel seen. In a world where most people are waiting for their turn to speak rather than truly listening, that kind of attention is rare. If you want to become a super connector, you must first become a disciplined listener.

Have you ever been at a conference where someone approaches you, hands you their business card before you even finish introducing yourself, and immediately begins telling you what they need? It feels transactional, almost invasive. There is no curiosity, or interest in your story, just urgency about theirs. Ironically, this approach produces the opposite of what they want. Instead of connection, it creates distance.

Most people approach networking with a subtle form of self-interest. They are thinking about how this person can help them, promote them, hire them, or elevate them. Very few enter a room asking, "How can I serve? What does this person need? Who might I connect them to?" That shift changes everything.

I want to challenge you, the next time you are in a room full of opportunity, resist the impulse to lead with your résumé. Instead, lead with curiosity. Ask a thoughtful question and listen without interruption.

Pay attention to what challenges they are facing. If you have a resource, idea or introduction that could genuinely help them, offer it, but as service, not as a tactic.

You might even set a quiet goal before entering the room: I will meaningfully help one to three people tonight – not collect fifteen shallow interactions or distribute twenty business cards, just one to three real conversations. Connection is not built through volume, it is built through presence.

THE COST OF DISCONNECTION

I once heard a story about a young stockbroker in New York who was aggressively building his career while unintentionally neglecting his family. He worked eighty-hour weeks. He left home at six in the morning and returned close to seven at night. Each evening, his six-year-old daughter would run to the door when she heard him enter. "Daddy, Daddy!" He would give her a quick greeting, then head straight to his home office to continue reviewing spreadsheets and quarterly reports.

One evening, she decided she would not let him slip past her again. When he walked in, she wrapped herself around his knees and refused to let go. After several minutes, he finally looked down and said, "Baby, what are you doing down there?" She looked up and said, "Daddy, I live down here." In that moment, he realized something devastating. His ambition had crowded out connection and his schedule had replaced presence. In focusing so much on performance, he had missed the chance to truly connect with his only child.

Connection is not just about listening long enough to respond, it is about stepping into another person's world with the intention of understanding it. It involves slowing down enough to learn someone's story, their hopes, fears, dreams and more. This requires empathy and curiosity. To do this you might have to practice maintaining eye contact instead of scanning the room for someone more "important" or putting your phone away instead of glancing at it mid-conversation. It is resisting the urge to think about what you are going to say next and instead listening fully to what is being said now. It's the discipline to care about someone else's story as much as you care about your own.

When done well, connection is mutually beneficial. You gain fulfillment by supporting someone else's vision. They gain validation and encouragement because they are heard. They leave the interaction encouraged rather than extracted from.

That is the principle of sowing and reaping at work. When you consistently invest attention, empathy, and support into others, you create relational equity that compounds over time. Value given returns as value multiplied.

This is why I intentionally avoid the word "networking" and prefer the word "connecting." Networking often carries the undertone of transaction. It implies, sometimes subtly and sometimes obviously, "What can this person do for me?" It is oriented around advancement, status, or expansion of influence.

Connecting is different. It asks, "How can I serve? How can I understand? How can we both grow from this interaction?" With that, super connectors are committed to cultivating relationships. They understand that genuine relationships are the real currency in life.

UNDERSTAND HOW YOU'RE WIRED

The cost of disconnection is subtle, but it compounds. It results in missed opportunities, shallow relationships, you'll find yourself in rooms, but never truly engaged. If you are going to accelerate your transition from student-athlete to professional, entrepreneur, or leader, you must learn to become a super connector. Beyond good listening, this skill requires interpersonal awareness, emotional intelligence, and cultural sensitivity.

However, before you can strengthen your connection with others, you must first understand yourself. Your natural wiring influences how you engage the world. Some people draw energy from conversation and move easily through rooms. Others prefer depth over volume and connect more meaningfully in one-on-one settings.

For example, extroverts tend to feel comfortable initiating conversations and meeting new people. They are often energized by interaction and can move fluidly from one person to the next. Introverts, on the other hand, may feel more energized in smaller settings and excel at deep, focused conversations with one individual at a time. Neither is better, they are simply different and becoming a super connector is possible for both.

Understanding your wiring helps you identify the obstacles you must overcome. If you are introverted, you may need to intentionally push yourself to speak up in larger spaces. If you are extroverted, you may need to discipline yourself to slow down and truly listen instead of dominating the exchange. Self-awareness prevents your strengths from turning into liabilities.

There are a number of practical tools that can help you gain this awareness. Assessments such as 5 Voices, the Enneagram, DISC, and Clifton StrengthsFinder can provide insight into how you naturally operate. What I appreciate about these tools is that they do not just focus on your individual traits. They reveal how you show up in a team environment. They also help you understand how others experience you when you collaborate, lead, or communicate under pressure.

Once you understand how you are wired, you can begin using that knowledge strategically. The goal is not to change who you are. The goal is to be intentional.

When you do make a connection, do not let it fade into a casual, "Let's stay in touch." That phrase rarely produces anything. If you exchange contact information, schedule the follow-up conversation before you leave. Put it on the calendar and create momentum.

Understanding how you are wired is the foundation of becoming a super connector. When you know yourself, you can stretch yourself. When you stretch yourself, your relationships expand with you.

HOW TO BECOME A SUPER CONNECTOR

Kobe Bryant once said, "The most important thing is to try and inspire people so that they can be great in whatever they want to do." Inspiration does not happen at a distance; it requires connection. If you want to become a super connector, here is how you begin.

1. TAKE INITIATIVE BY GOING FIRST

Do not wait for someone to approach you. One of the biggest mistakes people make in professional environments is assuming the right person will notice them. That someone will walk over and the right opportunity will introduce itself.

It rarely works that way.

If you want connection, take the first step. Walk up to someone introduce yourself, and ask a question that centers on them, not on you. Be proactive. Most people are waiting for someone else to make the first move. When you go first, you immediately separate yourself. Remember starting a conversation is not the goal, creating space for someone to share their story is. Super connectors are not the loudest voices in the room, they are often the most curious.

2. FIND COMMON GROUND

Connection accelerates when shared ground is discovered. Imagine two people stranded in a foreign country who cannot speak the local language. If they are both wearing Los Angeles Lakers jerseys, they have instantly found something familiar. That shared symbol becomes a bridge.

Common ground is all about establishing a shared language around experiences, upbringing, desires, hopes and dreams. While most people look for common ground in the past, I have found that the strongest bonds are often built around the future. For example, two families buying homes in the same new neighborhood, entrepreneurs launching businesses at the same time, or two students entering the same mastermind.

Once you identify what someone cares about and see where your paths cross, connection stops feeling forced and begins to happen naturally.

3. LISTEN TO HEAR, NOT TO RESPOND

We have already talked some about listening, but it deserves deeper attention. Most people believe they are good listeners. The truth is, we are often distracted, divided, or mentally preparing our response while someone else is still speaking. Research suggests that we retain only a small percentage of what we hear in conversation. Some studies indicate that we remember roughly 25 percent of what is said. Add to that the reality that the average human attention span has dropped to just a few seconds (often cited as shorter than that of a goldfish) and you begin to understand the challenge.

In a world full of noise, real listening is rare. So if you can grasp that skill, you'll have an advantage.

There is a difference between listening to hear and listening to respond. Listening to hear means your goal is understanding versus reacting. When you listen to respond, the conversation becomes centered on you. You interrupt, finish sentences, or jump ahead. You assume you know where the person is going before they get there. You may not intend to come across as dismissive, but that is often how it feels. I learned this the hard way.

When Covid-19 hit and Zoom became my new office, I realized my listening habits were not as strong as I thought. I would be on calls with my camera on, nodding at the right times, but I was also cooking, checking messages, and multitasking. I looked engaged, but I was only partially present.

To be clear, presence is not the same as attention. If you want to become a super connector, you must discipline yourself to slow down, let the person finish speaking, and process what was said before you respond.

One practical framework that has helped me is the OARS model.

- **O- Open-ended questions.** Ask questions that invite explanation, not just facts. Instead of "Did that go well?" ask, "What made that meaningful for you?" This allows the person who is speaking more room to share.

- **A- Affirmations.** Acknowledge what the person is feeling. Even if you do not agree with their perspective, affirm that you hear their experience. This may sound like, "I understand that this was a very difficult experience for you, and you feel..." It demonstrates empathy.

- **R- Reflection.** Restate what you heard in your own words. "What I'm hearing you say is..." This ensures clarity before you draw any conclusions and move forward.

- **S- Summaries.** Recap the main points and ask if you understood correctly. This might sound like "Okay, so my understanding is that you did A, B and C. Did I miss anything?" Give them the opportunity to correct you.

Using this method allows you to check your listening quality after someone has shared something with you. When someone feels heard, trust is built and connection deepens. If you want to stand out in this next season, do not just sharpen your résumé, sharpen your listening.

4. RELEASE EXPECTATIONS AND ASSUMPTIONS

Assumptions quietly sabotage connection. Stephen Covey once said, "We judge ourselves by our intentions and others by their behavior." That gap is where disconnection begins.

When you approach people with expectations already formed in your mind, you are not truly meeting them. You are meeting your version of them. Having your own expectations and assumptions can create subtle disconnection when you are trying to connect with someone.

For example, you might get into a car with someone and assume they want background music playing. You turn it on without asking. Meanwhile, they may prefer silence. What felt thoughtful to you may feel distracting to them. Or you might meet someone who speaks Spanish and assume they want to be greeted in their native language. You say, "Hola!" thinking you are being respectful, but they may reserve that language for intimate conversations with family and close friends. Your assumption, though well-intended, creates distance instead of closeness.

My encouragement is to always err on the side of asking rather than assuming. Replace "I know what they want" with "Help me understand what you prefer." That small shift preserves dignity and builds trust. Connection requires curiosity, not assumption.

Assumptions do not only show up in small moments, they can also show up in how we categorize people. Additionally, release your expectations. Allow every individual and relationship to stand on its own merits. Do not pre-define someone based on what you have heard about them or because they remind you of someone from your past.

When you do that, you never truly meet anyone for the first time. You are too busy filtering them through old experiences. You judge, assess, project, and operate with the assumption you already know who they are. When you assume you already know someone, you stop listening and your connection is impacted.

I once coached a young college student who could not understand why she kept attracting the same type of unhealthy relationship. Part of the issue may have been the men she was meeting, but another part was that her mind was constantly scanning for familiar traits from past experiences. She was looking for patterns she already knew. She was expecting repetition. The reality is what we look for we often find.

If you are going to become a super connector, you must discipline yourself to approach new relationships without the weight of old ones. That does not mean you ignore wisdom from the past. It means you refuse to let the past define the present. This may be easier said than done. It requires intentional effort and emotional maturity. Super connectors do not enter rooms with conclusions, they enter with questions and that posture changes everything.

RUN THIS PLAY

Start your journey as a super connector by writing about the following in your journal for the next 10 – 15 minutes:

- Many times, jobs are given to people from the same network. Who are 5 people within your network that you can leverage as you pursue new opportunities?

- What groups, clubs, religious groups, former teams, or schools that you attended can you leverage as you pursue new opportunities?

ACTION STEPS

Commit to taking the following actions this week. After you have completed each action, remember to write a few notes to remind yourself about the details of what you did, how it felt, and what additional follow-up needs to be done.

- Find a networking event in your area that suits your interests or passion. Before you attend, make sure you are properly prepared by doing the following:
  - Know the dress code and be professional.

- Have some copies of your resume on hand or print some business cards.
- Update your social media profiles, LinkedIn accounts, and all online platforms where you have a digital presence.
- Go to the networking event and make connections. Remember to leave the event with one coffee meeting or phone call on your calendar.

AFFIRMATION

Repeat this affirmation, while looking at yourself in the mirror, every day for the next 21 days:

"I am confident in my skills and expertise. I work well with others and contribute meaningfully to any team or organization I join."

PLAY #7:
CONNECT TO THE SOURCE

In the last chapter, we talked about becoming a super connector. While developing those skills and relationships are both important and valuable, over time I learned something important. You can be deeply connected to people and still feel internally disconnected. You can build a strong network and still feel spiritually dry.

As valuable as connection with others is, there is one relationship that anchors everything else: your connection with God. In transition, especially after sports, when everything shifts, the applause quiets, there's no routine and team, and all that remains is you, this truth becomes clear. You need something deeper than drive, you need a source.

For me, that source is God. I acknowledge some of you have walked closely with God for years. Some of you are questioning. Some of you are unsure what you believe and I respect that, but I would be doing you a disservice if I did not tell you plainly what carried me.

I refer to God as the Source because that has been my lived experience as I've walked with Jesus over the years. During one of the most overwhelming seasons of my life, I learned what it truly meant to draw from God.

I WAS EMOTIONALLY AND SPIRITUALLY DEHYDRATED

In my last year of college, once football season ended, I was overwhelmed. I was anxious about what would come next after football. I remember sending out job applications everywhere, hoping one of them would be the right one. I was preparing to graduate, but I still had classes to make up, so I was juggling that as well. It felt like everything was happening at once.

I was asking myself questions nonstop. Which job do I take? How do I apply myself in the professional world? What does life look like without the structure of football? There was so much to figure out and so much to manage. I was doing everything I could to stay on top of it, but mentally and emotionally, I was nearing burnout.

One afternoon, in the middle of that season, I went to visit my mentor, Dr. Keith Hall, in his office. The moment I walked in, he could tell something was off. He looked at me and asked a simple question: "What do you need right now?"

I answered honestly. "I just need rest. I'm tired." He had a long black leather couch in the corner of his office next to a small round table. Without hesitation, he told me to lie down. No lecture. No advice. No strategy session. Just rest.

As I lay there, something shifted. I distinctly remember sensing God's voice in that quiet moment, almost as if He was saying, *"Just rest in Me. You do not need to stress about what is next. You do not need to worry about the job, the graduation, the future. Just rest."*

Dr. Hall continued working at his desk while I lay there, eyes closed, emotionally exhausted. I broke down internally. I felt supported. I felt seen. I felt safe. It was as if God had used my mentor to create space for me to breathe. I remember thinking, *God has me. I can rest.*

I fell into one of the deepest sleeps I had experienced in months. When I woke up nearly an hour later, my first reaction was embarrassment. This was supposed to be a mentoring meeting. I was supposed to be sharp, attentive, and ready. Instead, I had taken a nap, but then clarity came. That rest was the meeting.

I left refreshed in a way that no productivity plan could have provided. God did not give me a five-step blueprint that afternoon. He gave me peace and he used my mentor to create space for that. It was exactly what I needed.

WHAT DO YOU NEED?

Has the end of your sports career placed you in a similar space? Are you trying to figure out school, graduation, résumé, job offers, relocation, finances, identity, all at once? I know how mentally and emotionally draining that can be. This is not just a tough season for athletes, it is a difficult transition for anyone stepping from one defined structure into uncertainty.

Maybe you feel overworked and overwhelmed. Maybe you feel like you are moving fast, but getting nowhere. Maybe the future intimidates you because it does not look the way you once imagined. Maybe you regret decisions you made and now feel like they are catching up to you. Or maybe you just feel alone and the question you have to ask yourself is "What do I really need right now?"

Whatever it is, here is the truth: you do not have to carry this all by yourself. Jesus said in Matthew 11:28, "Come to Me, all who are weary and burdened, and I will give you rest." It is an invitation from God. Why would you choose to manage transition alone when you have access to the Source?

There are needs in this season that strategy alone cannot solve. You were not designed to navigate uncertainty on willpower alone. This affirms a truth we often ignore, human beings were created with limits. We were not designed to carry the full weight of our own existence. Yet too often, we take everything onto ourselves. We shoulder the burden of our future or attempt to control outcomes we cannot see. We internalize stress, anxiety, and pressure as if it is normal. It is not. Operating under constant self-imposed pressure for long stretches of time will break you down mentally, emotionally, and spiritually. You were never meant to live in survival mode indefinitely.

One of the greatest dangers of not tapping into the Source is that your sanity eventually comes into question. When you believe everything depends on you, your performance, your decisions, your ability to "get it right", the weight becomes crushing. You live in quiet fear of making the wrong move , walking around tense, bracing for collapse. That is not strength, it is exhaustion disguised as responsibility.

That kind of pressure changes how you show up in dating relationships, friendships, at work, and in every environment you enter. The heavy burden of having to do everything "just right" begins to shape your personality. You become reactive and defensive instead of peaceful and grounded. That was never God's design.

YOU CAN DEPEND ON HIM.

Over the years, I have traveled to different countries, met people of different faith backgrounds, and had conversations across belief systems. Those experiences have strengthened, not weakened, my conviction. One of the most important things I have learned in my journey with God is this: He expects us to depend on Him. He desires to be our Provider, our Protector, and our Peace Giver. He does not ask us to carry our own future. He invites us to trust Him with it. Proverbs 3:5 says, "Trust in the Lord and lean not on your own understanding..."

The tension is that most of us understand this intellectually, but we do not live it internally. We say we belong to God, we trust Him, and we are His sons and daughters, but when pressure rises, we default to self-reliance. We begin striving or trying to make things happen. We begin carrying burdens that were never ours to carry and without realizing it, we start living like spiritual orphans.

When we shift our dependence from God to ourselves, fear follows, anxiety increases, and restlessness grows. We try to control outcomes we cannot see, but when we trust Him, our experience is altogether different. We receive peace, rest, and assurance even in the face of uncertainty. The difference is not in the circumstance, it is in the source of dependence.

In 2018, after graduating from APU, I began working at the university as a campus pastor's assistant and as a graduate assistant in the campus pastor's office. I was mentoring small group leaders, coordinating chapel services, helping manage ministry events, and stepping into leadership in ways that stretched me. It was meaningful work, but it was also a season where I was learning how to depend on God in a new way outside of football.

One event stands out. APU hosted an annual outreach called "Night of Champions," where thousands of young athletes from the community would come to campus for a day of games, food, and ultimately, a testimony from a Christian athlete. My role that evening was to host the green room backstage, welcoming the guest speaker, creating a peaceful environment, and making sure everything ran smoothly.

That year, the guest athlete was Olympic gold medalist Allyson Felix. As we waited backstage, I asked her a question that had been on my mind. "When did you know you were going to win the race where you broke the record?" She looked at me calmly and said, "I knew well before I started." She explained that she had already seen the outcome internally. In her spiritual imagination, the victory was settled. She trusted that she had done the preparation, and she depended completely on God for the result. By the time race day came, the win was not a surprise; it was confirmation. That conversation stayed with me.

Allyson trained hard, she prepared relentlessly, but she understood something deeper: preparation without dependence is incomplete. She did her part, but she trusted God with what she could not control.

That is what it looks like to depend on Him. You cannot accelerate your transition if you are mentally and emotionally exhausted from trying to control everything. You cannot perform at your highest level if your spirit is depleted. I dare you to surrender your need to control outcomes, your need to look impressive, your obsession with getting it perfect.

Here is what I know from experience: when you tap into God and rely on His power, He refreshes you in ways you did not even realize you needed. He brings the right people into your life at the right time. He opens doors you could not have forced open. He provides resources and clarity that accelerate your transition far beyond what your effort alone could accomplish. Like Allyson, you also have access to the power of imagination. The difference is how you choose to use it.

Up until now, you may have been using your imagination to rehearse fear. *What if I get no Division I offers? What if my test scores are not high enough? What if I get injured? What if no one hires me? What if I fail?* Over and over again, your mind runs negative scenarios, preparing for outcomes you hope never happen, but what if you redirected that same imagination toward faith?

What would it look like to use "What if?" as a doorway to possibility instead of a trigger for anxiety? *What if this door opens? What if the right opportunity finds me? What if God positions me in a place I never could have engineered on my own?*

One word I treat like a curse in my own mind is the word *can't*. The moment "I can't" enters the conversation, growth stops, but when you replace "I can't" with "How can I?" your thinking expands and when you are connected to God, you are not asking that question alone. You are partnering your preparation with His power.

HOW TO CONNECT TO THE SOURCE:

This is the most important connection you will ever build and like anything that matters, it requires intention. Depending on God is not passive, it's a partnership.

1. DO YOUR PART FIRST

When I say tap into God's power, I mean this: do everything within your capacity and then release what is beyond your control. Go to class. Finish strong. Apply for the job. Take the internship. Make the call. Send the email. Build the résumé. Have the meeting. Put in the work.

Trusting God does not mean doing nothing, sitting back, folding your arms, and waiting for heaven to drop an opportunity on your doorstep while you binge-watch and scroll. Once you've done your part, stop carrying the outcome like it rests entirely on your shoulders. To be clear, God is not asking you to replace effort with passivity; He is asking you to replace anxiety with trust. There is a difference.

But first, you cannot expect direction from Someone you are disconnected from. It's important to get planted in a local church. Find a smaller community where you can be known, challenged, and encouraged. Creating connection also looks like making space in your week to meet with God consistently. High performers are used to grinding without pause, but your spirit needs rhythm. Whether it is a walk by the water, a quiet corner in a park, or a hike where you can breathe and think clearly, create space to recharge. Even a Tesla cannot make the drive from San Diego to San Francisco without stopping to charge. You are no different. If you want to go far, you must stay filled.

Finally, serve. Find a way to contribute that is not centered on your platform, your performance, or your resume. When you serve others, you are reminded that your value is not confined to a scoreboard. There is something spiritually grounding about losing yourself in service. It recalibrates your heart and keeps you aligned with what actually matters.

2. RELEASE YOURSELF FROM THE RESPONSIBILITY OF BEING YOUR OWN SAVIOR

After you have done what you can, let God make the final call. This is where most people struggle. We can work hard, but we do not like surrendering control.

If the opportunity comes, receive it with gratitude. If it does not, trust that the closed door is as intentional as the open one. That job you wanted but did not get? It may have been protection. You can do what is legal, ethical, and within your power to create income, opportunity, and growth, but do not do it in a state of internal chaos. If you are walking with God and aligning your life with His principles, you are not alone in the process, He sees you, He is for you, and He is capable of orchestrating outcomes you could never engineer by yourself. When you understand that God is a Father who takes responsibility for His children, you are secure, and not driven by fear or worry.

3. SPEAK YOUR SURRENDER ALOUD, THEN REST

Surrender is not just a thought. It is a declaration. After you decide that you are going to trust God, say it, pray it, and speak it out loud. There is something powerful about moving trust from your head into your words. It marks a decision. Once you decide to trust God, rest in that.

Rest from the obsession of managing every detail, the illusion that your effort alone determines your future, and the anxiety of unanswered questions. You will still have gaps. You will not know every step. The end of your sports career may still feel uncertain, but uncertainty does not mean abandonment. It means you are walking by faith. A simple prayer might sound like this:

"God, thank You for reminding me that I am not alone. You created me to depend on You, not to carry my future by myself. I have done what I can to prepare. The rest is in Your hands. I surrender my need to control outcomes. If You open the door, I will walk through it. If You close it, I will trust You. I rely on Your strength, not my own. I rest in You. Amen."

This is how you connect to the Source. You prepare with excellence, align your life, release control, declare your surrender, and then you rest. From that place, you do not just transition, you accelerate.

RUN THIS PLAY

Connect to the source by writing about the following in your journal for the next 10 – 15 minutes:

- **What do you honestly need from God right now?**

  Is it clarity? Peace? Provision? Confidence? Direction? Courage? Name it specifically.

- **In what ways has God uniquely gifted you?**

  List at least five. Think beyond talent. Consider your personality, your resilience, your leadership, your ability to encourage, your discipline, your creativity. Where do you consistently see evidence of grace on your life?

- **What major responsibilities have you been trying to carry alone?**

  Identify the weight. Where have you assumed full control instead of shared dependence?

- **Where in your life are you feeding fear instead of faith?**

  Be specific. What thoughts keep repeating? What worst-case scenarios are you rehearsing? What is getting in the way of deeper trust?

- Death and life are in the power of your tongue. **What areas of your life would you like to speak life into?**

ACTION STEPS

Commit to completing the following actions this week. After you finish each one, remember to write a few notes about what you experienced, what stood out to you, and any follow-up you need to take. Growth happens when reflection follows action.

- **SPEAK LIFE INTENTIONALLY**

Read Proverbs 18:21 aloud in multiple translations. Reflect on what God is speaking to you through them.

"The tongue has the power of life and death."

"The stakes are high. Your words can either speak life, or your words can speak death."

Ask yourself:

- Where have my words been building?
- Where have they been tearing down?
- What is God prompting me to change?

Write what you sense God highlighting.

- **PLANT A SEED OF FAITH**

Faith is often compared to a seed, something small that, when planted and nurtured, grows over time.

This week, go to a local store and buy a simple plant and potting mix. Plant it in your home or yard. As you water it and watch it grow over the next few weeks, reflect on this principle: what you sow consistently is what you eventually reap.

Pay attention to the parallels between the natural process and your spiritual life.

- What seeds are you planting through your thoughts?
- Through your words?
- Through your habits?

Write down what this visual reminder teaches you.

AFFIRMATION

Repeat this affirmation, while looking at yourself in the mirror, every day for the next 21 days:

"I am worthy. I am prized. I have what it takes."

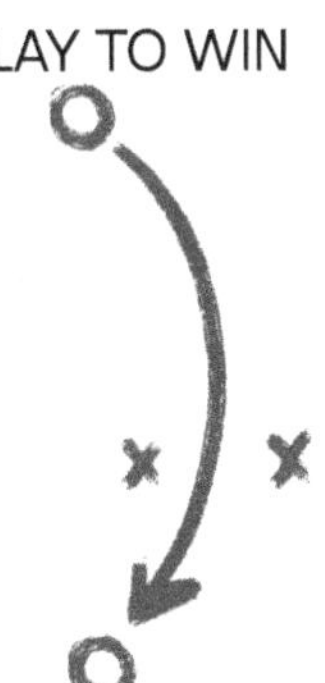

PLAY #8:
PLAY TO WIN

There is a distinct difference between playing to win and playing not to lose, and if you have competed long enough, you have felt it in your body. Playing not to lose is cautious and tight; it is when you stop attacking and start protecting, when the fear of making a mistake becomes louder than the desire to make a play.

Playing to win, on the other hand, is disciplined, but bold. It trusts preparation, executes with confidence, and refuses to shrink in the moment. As we close this book and you step into the next season of your life, this distinction matters more than ever. The uniform may come off, the crowd may disappear, and the structure of your sport may fade, but the question remains: will you approach life protecting yourself from failure, or will you choose to build it with the same courage and intentionality you once brought to competition? Will you play to win?

WHEN PREPARATION PAYS OFF

I was a champion at all three levels of competition: High School, Junior College, and NCAA. I won a state CIF championship in football, broke the 4 x 100 record for track and field at my high school, won a bowl game in junior college at Riverside Community College, and won back-to-back Division 2 GNAC championships at Azusa Pacific University, the first time this occurred in the school's history.

To this day, I still remember playing for Corona Centennial High School and being in Carson, California where we won a state championship against De La Salle High School. Holding up that big championship trophy with the state of California engraved on it made me feel like I'd won the lotto! I can't help but think about that championship without automatically thinking about all of the intense preparation that went into getting ready for it. We worked really hard for that win. We practiced every day and then competed at a high level. The last practice of the week leading up to the state championship was especially memorable. I vividly recall how it was pouring down rain and freezing cold. I mean, it was so cold that when it wasn't our turn to practice on the field, we were all hugged up against each other on the sidelines trying to warm ourselves with each other's body heat. We stayed out there practicing for hours from afternoon until it was dark. Eventually, we had to go into the gym to practice because it was so cold and practiced until eight or nine o'clock at night. Then, a day or two later, we won the championship. It was a very close game, and we won by only a small margin of two points, but it was by far the biggest win of my life!

Once the clock ran out and it was official that our team had won the game, I jumped on my teammate's shoulders. The media actually took a picture of the moment and ran it on the front page of the local newspaper. Each time I looked at that picture, all I could think about was that long, wet, freezing-cold practice that we had to go through leading up to the big game, and all I could think was "Oh, my goodness, that practice was SO hard!" How the practice prepared us for victory was not lost on me. The reason we had won the game was because we were willing to prepare ourselves mentally and then physically by going through that gruesome practice. We also prepared ourselves emotionally by being confident and ready to play. It wasn't preparation in one area that led to victory, it was preparation in every area.

Over time, I've learned this is also the case for life after sports. Preparation is correlated to success. My pastor always says preparation is prophetic. In other words, how you prepare today is a declaration of what you believe about tomorrow. When you prepare with intention, you are signaling that you expect something greater ahead. You are aligning your habits with the future you say you want. The way we practiced before that championship game revealed what we believed was possible. In the same way, the way you prepare now reveals what you believe about your own life.

MEDIOCRITY IS A DECISION

If preparation reveals what you believe about your future, then mediocrity reveals something too. It reveals a quiet decision about what you think is possible for your life. You don't drift into average by accident. You arrive there through repeated choices, lowering the standard, avoiding the stretch, and protecting comfort instead of pursuing growth. Mediocrity is not usually the result of a lack of ability; it is the result of a belief that says, "This is enough," when deep down you know you were built for more.

The truth is, most people don't consciously choose mediocrity, they arrive there slowly. Life is demanding, transitions are exhausting, expectations stack up and you get tired. In culture, there's constant anxiety, pressure, and comparison. No wonder comfort and familiarity start to feel like the better choice. With that, life becomes more about managing fear and fatigue. Kobe Bryant once said, "Rest at the end, not in the middle." That statement wasn't about ignoring fatigue; it was about refusing to let exhaustion redefine your standard. There is a difference between healthy rest and quiet resignation. One restores you so you can continue building. The other convinces you to lower the ceiling.

When you stop preparing with intention, your energy doesn't disappear, it just gets redirected. Instead of building vision, you start managing anxiety.

Instead of imagining possibility, you rehearse worst-case scenarios. Rather than using your imagination for victory, it has already decided what defeat will look and feel like for you. The reality is, your mind is never idle. If you are not deliberately leading it toward growth, it will default toward self-protection.

Neuroscience reveals how the brain often cannot distinguish between a vividly imagined experience and a real one. In other words, when you repeatedly rehearse failure in your mind, your body responds as if it is already happening. There is another phenomenon psychologists mention called cognitive bias. This is the tendency of the mind to search for evidence that confirms what it already believes. If you believe you are stuck, your brain will find proof. If you believe you are limited, it will highlight limitations. If you believe average is acceptable, it will justify average. So if your mind is going to rehearse something anyway, why train it to expect collapse instead of possibility? Why allow bias to confirm mediocrity when you could discipline it toward belief?

The battle between playing to win and playing not to lose is rarely external first. It is internal. It begins with what you believe is possible, what you repeatedly picture, and what standard you decide to live by.

THE WINNING STANDARD

Once that decision is made internally, it must be expressed externally. Winning in life does not happen by accident. It is the result of a standard. Every championship team operates by one. There is a level of effort that is expected. A level of discipline that is normal. A level of preparation that is non-negotiable. Nobody debates the standard because it is understood. It is reinforced and protected.

If you want to accelerate your transition from student-athlete to life beyond the game, and truly win in life, you must intentionally build the mentality, habits, relationships, and systems that support winning. Victory does not respond to wishful thinking. You cannot hope your way into success or drift into purpose. You must plan for it, prepare for it, and surround yourself with a culture that reinforces it. You must establish your winning standard.

Consider these questions:Have you actually envisioned your future? Do you clearly see where you want to go and who you want to become? Have you identified the steps required to get there? Look at your environment: Who are you around daily? Are they building? Growing? Pushing? Or are they waiting to see what life hands them? What mentors are guiding you? What skills are you sharpening? What rooms are you putting yourself in? These questions are not theoretical, they are practical and they matter for your future.

If you want to raise and protect your standard, anchor it in these three commitments:

1. SURROUND YOURSELF WITH WINNERS.

The company you keep will either reinforce your standard or quietly lower it. You cannot build a championship life in isolation. You need proximity to people who are striving, disciplined, and forward-moving. Surround yourself with individuals who either share your hunger for growth or are further ahead so you have something to chase. Standards rise in environments of accountability. When you are around people who expect excellence, you begin expecting it from yourself. This is one of the fastest ways to elevate your life.

2. CREATE A WINNING CULTURE.

Championship teams don't just have talented players, they have culture. Culture is built through daily disciplines, reinforced habits, and shared expectations. If you want to live at a higher standard, design an environment that supports it. Study what effective, high-performing people do and implement those practices. Celebrate small wins and normalize growth. Try speaking to yourself like someone who expects victory, not someone who hopes for it. Remember your standard becomes your default. So, reinforce the narrative that you are a winner and that all you do is win, win, win! Ensure that this narrative is reinforced in your words to yourself and others.

3. FOLLOW THROUGH.

Principles only work when applied. Everything in this book is an accelerator, but only if you use it. If you commit to these practices, you will increase your clarity, expand your opportunities, strengthen your performance, and become a positive force in your community, but the key is commitment.

Even writing this book required that same mentality. I wanted to write it for a long time, but desire alone does not produce results. I had to raise my own standard. I had to sit down, push through distraction, and commit to finishing what I started. It wasn't convenient or easy, but I kept my eyes on the outcome. Helping athletes navigate this transition with clarity and conviction is the end game. The fact that you are holding this book is evidence that preparation, when paired with commitment and a winning environment, produces victory.

Playing to win is a decision. Preparation is a decision. Excellence is a decision and the standard you hold is a decision. The uniform may be off. The crowd may be gone. The scoreboard may not be visible anymore, but the game is still being played.

So the final question is this:

Are you ready for your next play?

Let's go!

RUN THIS PLAY

Prepare to win by writing about the following in your journal for the next 10 – 15 minutes:

JOURNAL PROMPTS

- When you look at the people you spend the most time with, are they reinforcing your winning standard or quietly lowering it? In what specific ways are they building you up or getting in your way?

- After reading this book, what is one concrete way you will prepare differently for your next season? Be specific. What habit will you change, what environment will you shift, or what standard will you raise?

- What has been the most valuable insight or shift for you while engaging with this book? How will you apply it immediately rather than simply appreciating it?

ACTION STEPS

Commit to completing the following this week. Winning is built in repetition, not inspiration.

- Write down three wins from your week, small or large. Train your mind to recognize progress, not just perfection.
- Write down three things you are grateful for that money cannot buy and no one can take away from you. Gratitude stabilizes your mindset and strengthens your standard.

AFFIRMATION

For the next 21 days, stand in front of a mirror and say this aloud with conviction:

"I trust the process. I prepare with excellence. I hold a winning standard. I am positioned exactly where I need to be, and I move forward with confidence."

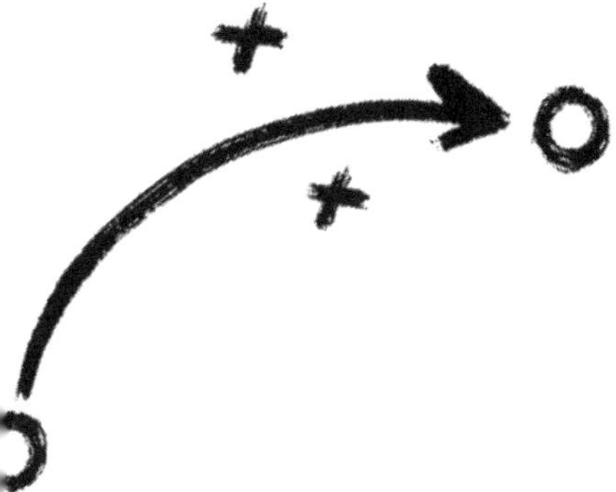

CHEAT SHEETS

QUICK REFERENCES FOR YOUR NEXT PLAY

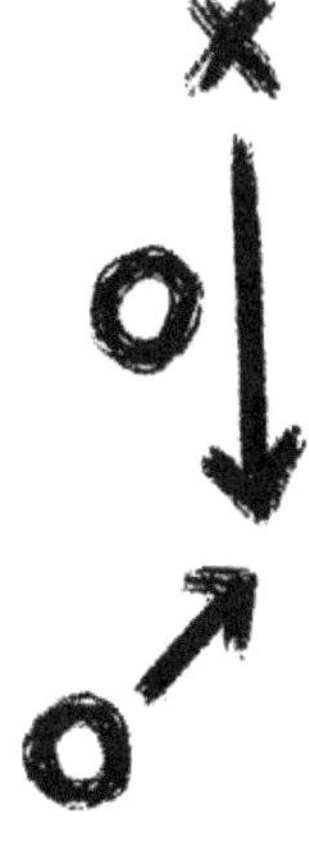

THE 8 PLAYS QUICK REFERENCE GUIDE

Think of this as your locker-room cheat sheet. When life gets loud, come back here.

PLAY #1: START WHERE YOU ARE

This moment matters. Before you run your next play, step fully off the last field. Be honest about where you are, not where you wish you were. Clarity starts with honesty, and honesty builds momentum.

PLAY #2: LEVERAGE YOUR PAIN

Don't waste what hurt. When you face it honestly, It reveals what mattered, what shaped you, and what still needs healing. Let pain refine you, not define you.

PLAY #3: DEVELOP YOUR IDENTITY

You are more than your sport. Performance was something you did, not who you are. Build an identity rooted in purpose, values, and character. Identity anchored internally survives external change.

PLAY #4: TRY SOMETHING NEW

Growth requires experimentation. Explore new skills, environments, and opportunities. The willingness to be a beginner again is a competitive advantage.

PLAY #5: DON'T LOSE YOUR EDGE

Discipline built your success in sports, it must follow you into this season. Keep training your mind, habits, and body. Maintain standards. Protect your edge.

PLAY #6: BECOME A SUPER CONNECTOR

Winning in life requires relationships. Learn to connect intentionally. Listen deeply. Understand how you're wired. Add value before asking for it.

PLAY #7: CONNECT TO THE SOURCE

Do your part, then release control. Depend on God as your Provider, Protector, and Peace Giver. Rest in Him. Align your preparation with surrender. Spiritual strength fuels sustainable success.

PLAY #8: PLAY TO WIN

Refuse mediocrity. Raise your standard. Build a winning culture around your life. Discipline your imagination toward belief. Surround yourself with winners. Execute daily.

AFFIRMATIONS FOR DAILY WINS

Read these aloud daily. Confidence is built through repetition.

IDENTITY & PURPOSE

- I am more than my performance.
- My identity is rooted in purpose, not applause.
- I am becoming who I was created to be.
- I start where I am and move forward with clarity.
- I refuse to live beneath my potential.

FAITH & DEPENDENCE

- God is my Source, my strength, and my peace.
- I do my part with excellence and trust God with the outcome.
- I release anxiety and receive rest.
- I surrender control and embrace clarity.
- I am never alone in this transition.
-

DISCIPLINE & PREPARATION

- I prepare daily because I expect to win.
- I do not lose my edge when the spotlight fades.

- Discipline follows me into every season.
- I celebrate small wins while pursuing bigger ones.
- I hold myself to a winning standard.

MINDSET & CONFIDENCE

- My imagination works for me, not against me.
- I replace "I can't" with "How can I?"
- I leverage pain for growth.
- I grow through discomfort.
- I refuse mediocrity.

RELATIONSHIPS & IMPACT

- I listen deeply and connect intentionally.
- I surround myself with people who raise my standard.
- I release assumptions and choose understanding.
- I add value in every room I enter.
- I am building a life of impact and influence.

ABOUT THE AUTHOR

HI, I'M DEJI (DAY-GEE)

Deji Olajide knows what it feels like when the game ends. As a former NCAA athlete who won CIF and state championships at Corona Centennial High School and later two NCAA Division II national championships in college, Deji understands the discipline, pressure, and identity that come with competing at a high level. He also understands the quiet tension that follows when the season closes and the spotlight fades. That transition changed his life.

What began as a personal journey to rediscover purpose beyond performance has become a calling; helping athletes navigate life after sports with clarity, faith, and confidence. Deji is passionate about walking with athletes through one of the most overlooked and emotionally complex seasons of their lives, the shift from student-athlete to professional, entrepreneur, or leader.

He holds a Bachelor of Arts in Sports Ministry and a Master of Divinity from Azusa Pacific University and is a certified coach through the Session 5 Institute and transformational trainer through GAP Community.

Since 2019, he has served as a sports chaplain for La Salle High School and Chaffey College, mentoring and developing student-athletes on and off the field. He also serves as a youth minister at Victory Bible Church, investing in the spiritual and personal growth of the next generation.

As a coach and speaker, Deji has worked with individuals and organizations across Los Angeles, Texas,

Maryland, Canada, Kenya, Nigeria, and Zambia. His work centers on identity development, purpose discovery, faith integration, leadership growth, and building the habits necessary to win in life, not just in sports.

If you are an athlete navigating transition, someone seeking clarity, or a leader ready to raise your standard, Deji would be honored to walk with you.

To book Deji for coaching, mentorship, or speaking engagements, visit dejiolajide.com or connect via email or social media.
deji@session5institute.com
@dejiolajide_

Your next play is waiting.